MAGIC EYE®

Amazing 3D Illusions
25th Anniversary Book

by Magic Eye Inc.

Andrews McMeel
PUBLISHING®

Andrews McMeel Publishing
a division of Andrews McMeel Universal
1130 Walnut Street, Kansas City, Missouri 64106

www.andrewsmcmeel.com

ISBN: 978-1-4494-9423-0

Library of Congress Control Number: 2018940287

22 23 24 25 26 SDB 12 11 10 9 8

Magic Eye Inc. 3D Images, Layout and Design: Cheri Smith, Catherine Smith, Sam Jones

2D Clipart & Photo Credits: © Cheri Smith, © Magic Eye Inc., Image(s) Licensed by Ingram Image, © clipart.com, a division of Getty Images, © clipart.com, a division of Vital Imagery Ltd., © Custom Thinkstock.

Disclaimer: The information contained in this book is intended to be educational and entertaining and is not for diagnosis, prescription, or treatment of any eye conditions or disease or any health disorder whatsoever. This information should not replace competent optometric or medical care. The author is in no way liable for any use or misuse of this material. Our wish is that further research will help to unlock the mystery of how vision and the brain work.

Magic Eye® images are available for educational, business, or sales promotional use. For information, please contact:

Magic Eye Inc., P.O. Box 1986, Provincetown, MA 02657
Tel: (508) 487-8484 Email: 3d@magiceye.com
www.magiceye.com

Visit our online store at
www.magiceyebooks.com

INTRODUCTION

It has been twenty-five years since Magic Eye® 3D products ignited the worldwide 3D craze of the 1990s! This book celebrates this milestone and offers a fascinating selection of Magic Eye 3D images. Each image features the latest 3D illusion advancements by the owner of Magic Eye Inc. and cocreator of Magic Eye 3D Images, Cheri Smith, and her supportive staff. This collection includes many images from the most recent award-winning Magic Eye wall calendars.

The spellbinding Magic Eye products have received many accolades, some of which are cited below.

Magic Eye Bestselling Books

When the first Magic Eye book was released in the United States in 1993, the response was as magical as the 3D images emerging from their colorful backgrounds. Viewers could not purchase these bestselling books fast enough. In fact, Magic Eye I, II, and III appeared on the *New York Times* bestseller list for a combined seventy-three weeks.

Internationally, Magic Eye books broke numerous bestseller list records as well. In 1995, the book *Magic Eye: A New Way of Looking at the World* had outsold any other book in German publishing history.

To date, twenty-nine Magic Eye books have been published and over twenty million Magic Eye books have been sold in more than twenty-five languages.

Amusing Stories from the 1990s

Many people are astonished when they first view a Magic Eye 3D image. The experience is unique and magical, and in the early '90s it seemed everyone had a Magic Eye story to share. Responses ranged from the enthusiastic "I see it!" to the exasperated "I don't see it. Are you making it up?"

In Japan, Magic Eye products were featured in many stores, including a magic store in Tokyo Disneyland. Magic Eye product areas were a popular place for teenage boys to assist teenage girls to "see 3D" and sometimes to get a date.

A favorite Magic Eye story involves a film crew from New Zealand. They were interviewing the staff of Magic Eye when they mentioned they had been filming an Aboriginal tribe in the outback of Australia the previous week. No one had met or filmed this tribe before. They felt honored when they were invited into an Aboriginal hut; and, to their surprise, hanging on the wall was a Magic Eye poster.

The owners of Magic Eye also received a call from the CIA, informing them their "secret messages" were under investigation.

Syndication & the Media

Countless newspapers, magazines, and radio and TV shows have featured Magic Eye images, including: *People* magazine, the *National Enquirer*, *USA Today*, the *Daily Mail* (UK), and *Der Spiegel* (Germany). From 1994 to present, Magic Eye weekly syndicated images have appeared in the comics section of numerous Sunday newspapers worldwide. Do you have a Magic Eye 3D image hidden in your newspaper?

TV show features or mentions include: *The Ellen Show*, *Seinfeld*, *Jeopardy!*, *Live! with Regis and Kelly*, *The Tonight Show*, *The Simpsons*, *This Is Us*, *Modern Family*, and *The Late Show with Stephen Colbert*, to name a few.

Creating a Magic Eye 3D Illusion

Creating a Magic Eye 3D illusion takes a combination of advanced technology and artistic ability. Magic Eye Inc. uses its own programs and innovative 3D techniques, and the result is a genuine Magic Eye® image.

Then and Now

Magic Eye 3D images were used to sell or promote just about everything in the '90s. These captivating images were printed on a wide variety of products, including posters, calendars, cereal boxes, soup and beverage labels, movie posters, and even bubble gum.

Maybe you own one of our favorite classic products, including the *Disney's Magic Eye* book, *Magic Eye: The Amazing Spider-Man* book, or the *Star Wars 1995 3D Calendar*.

Today, popular uses for Magic Eye images continue to include retail products, advertising, and promotions. Magic Eye 3D illustrations are highly sought after for entertainment, mindfulness practices, books, and magazines.

Magic Eye 3D May Improve Vision

Vision therapists worldwide have proven that Magic Eye images are useful for vision therapy. Viewing Magic Eye images may improve overall vision and reduce computer eyestrain. Four Magic Eye vision-improvement books have been published to date.

www.magiceye.com

To learn more about Magic Eye, visit the Magic Eye website. Here you can learn the science and history behind Magic Eye images and techniques, enter contests, view Magic Eye images, visit their online stores, and select links to Magic Eye social media sites.

If you are viewing Magic Eye 3D illusions for the first time, be certain to follow the viewing instructions on page 4.

It is the love of art and fun entertainment that motivates the owner of Magic Eye Inc. It is her wish that you will smile and be captivated by this latest collection of Magic Eye 3D images.

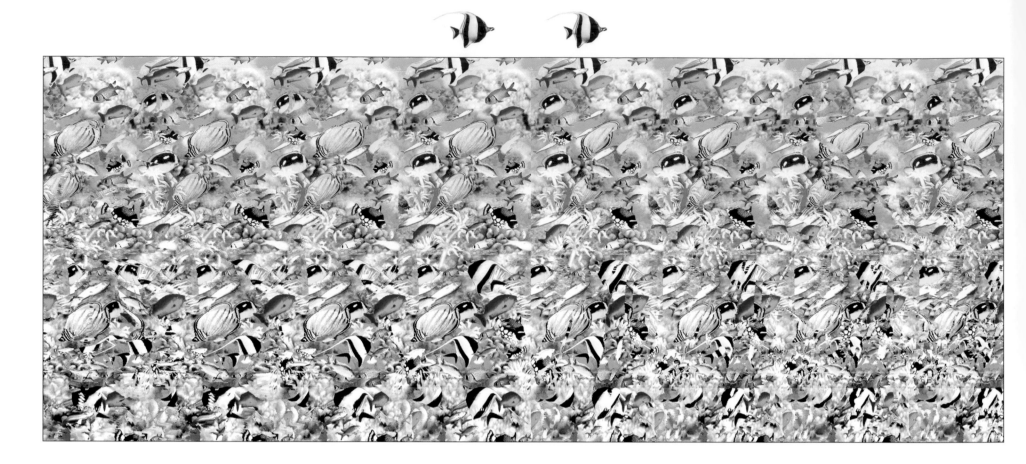

There are two methods for viewing Magic Eye images: diverging your eyes (focusing beyond the image) and converging your eyes (focusing before the image or crossing your eyes). All of the Magic Eye images in this book have been created to be viewed by diverging your eyes.

Instructions #1 for Diverging Your Eyes
(focusing beyond the image)

To reveal the hidden 3D illusion, hold the center of the image *right up to your nose*. It should be blurry. Focus as though you are looking *through* the image into the distance. *Very slowly* move the image away from your face until the two angelfish above the image turn into three angelfish. If you see four angelfish, move the image farther away from your face until you see three angelfish. If you see one or two angelfish, start over!

When you *clearly see three angelfish*, hold the page still, and the hidden image will slowly appear. Once you perceive the hidden image and depth, you can look around the entire 3D image. The longer you look, the clearer it becomes. The farther away you hold the page, the deeper it becomes.

Instructions #2 for Diverging Your Eyes
(focusing beyond the image)

To reveal the hidden 3D illusion, hold the center of this image *right up to your nose*. It should be blurry. Focus as though you are looking *through* the image into the distance. *Very slowly* move the image away from your face until you begin to perceive depth. Now hold the page still and the hidden image will slowly appear.

Magic Eye "Floaters"

Magic Eye "Floaters" are another type of Magic Eye 3D illusion. Floaters can first be viewed in 2D, then, by using the standard Magic Eye viewing techniques, Floaters will appear to float in 3D space. Floaters and Magic Eye hidden illusions may be combined. (See page 35).

Additional Viewing Information

Discipline is needed when a Magic Eye 3D illusion starts to "come in" because at that moment you will instinctively try to look at the page rather than looking through it or before it. If you "lose it," start again.

If you converge your eyes (focus before the image or cross your eyes) and view an image created for diverging your eyes, the depth information comes out backward, and vice versa! This means if we intend to show an airplane flying in front of a cloud, if you converge your eyes you will see an airplane-shaped hole cut into the cloud! Another common occurrence is to diverge or converge your eyes twice as far as is needed to see the hidden image. For example, when you see four squares above the image instead of three. In this case, you will see a scrambled version of the intended hidden image.

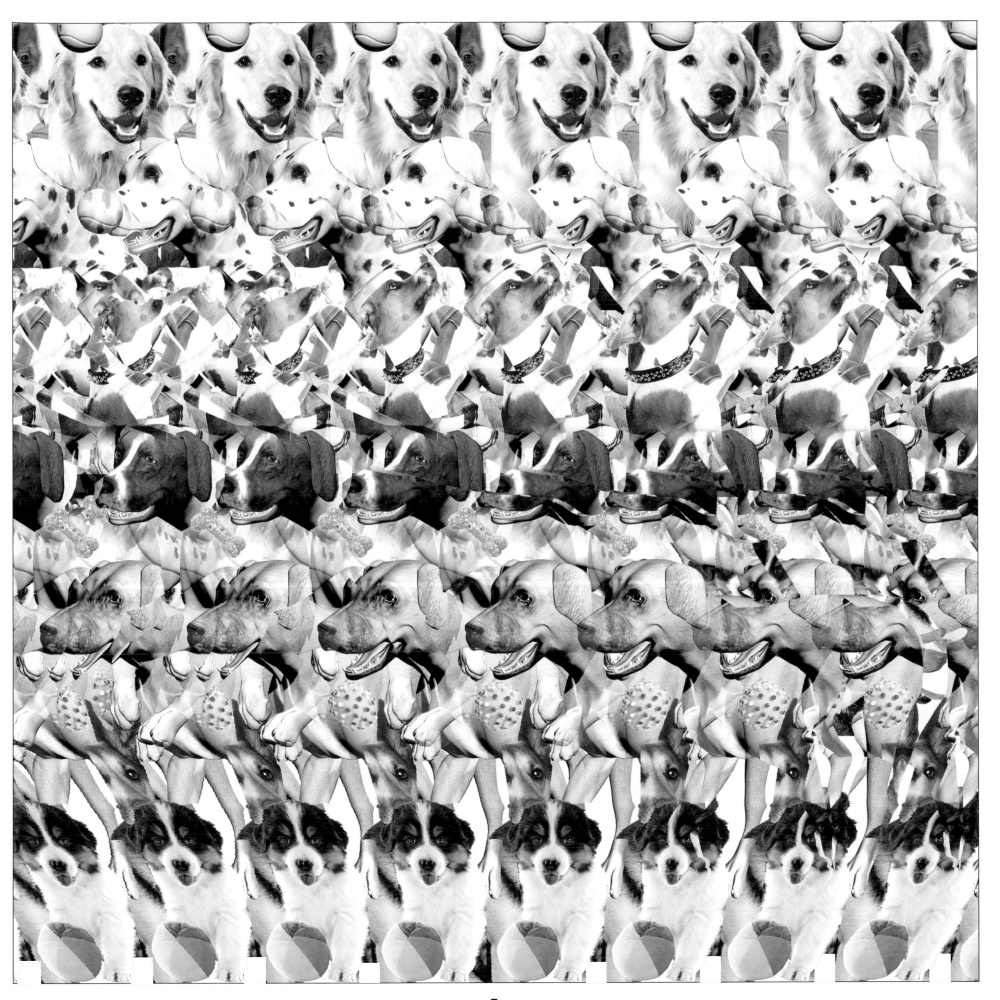

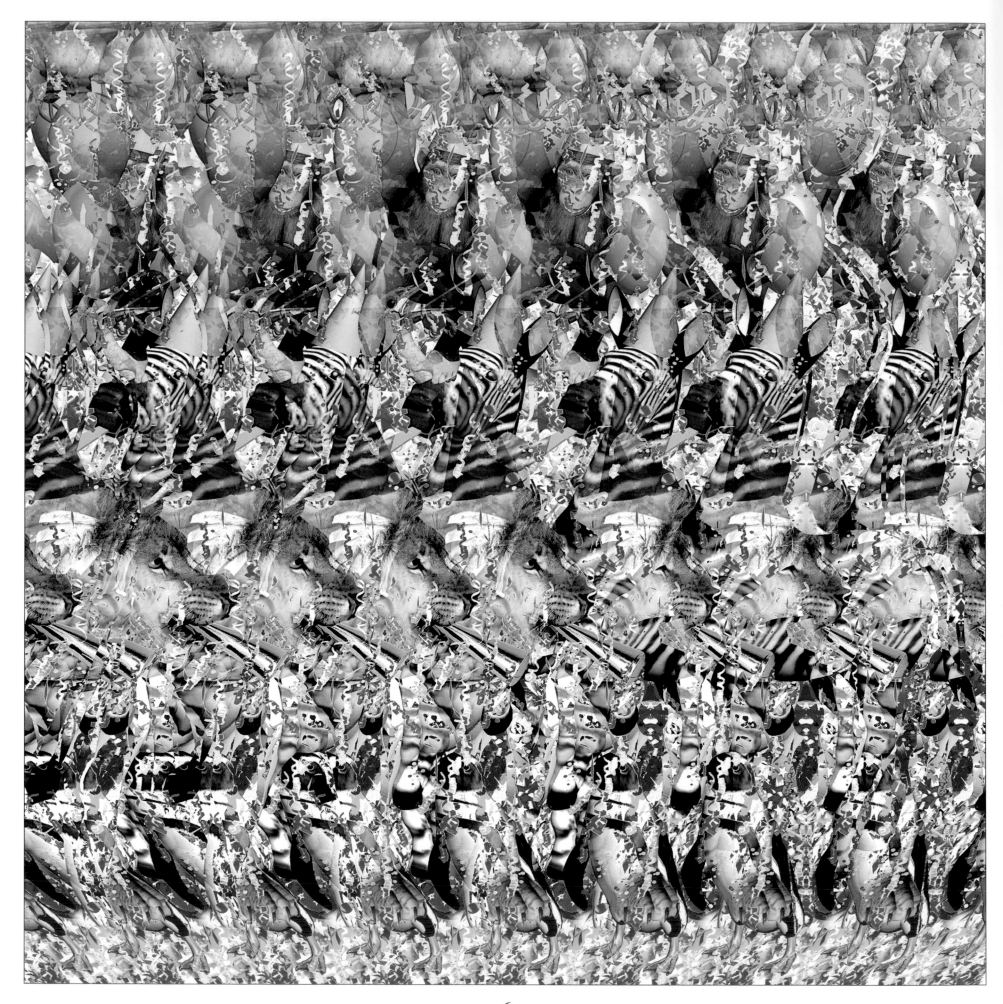

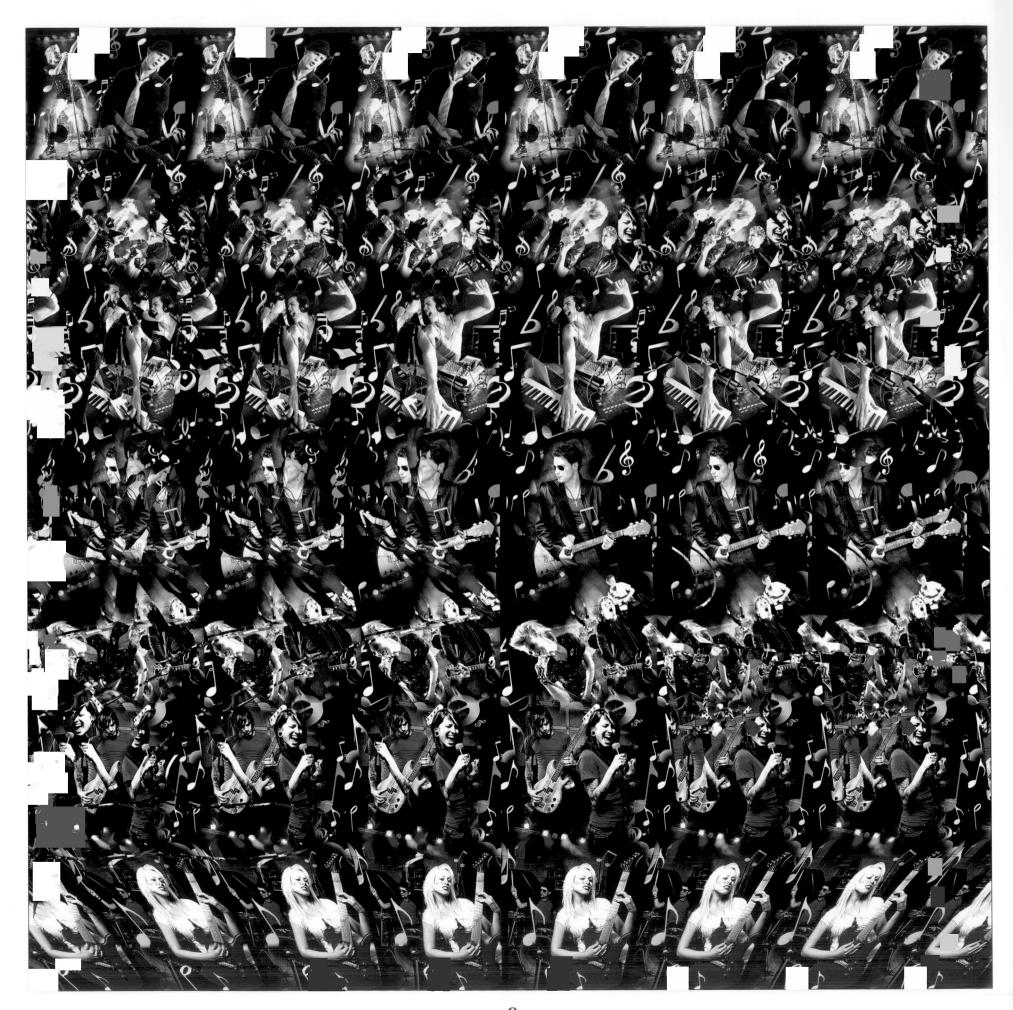

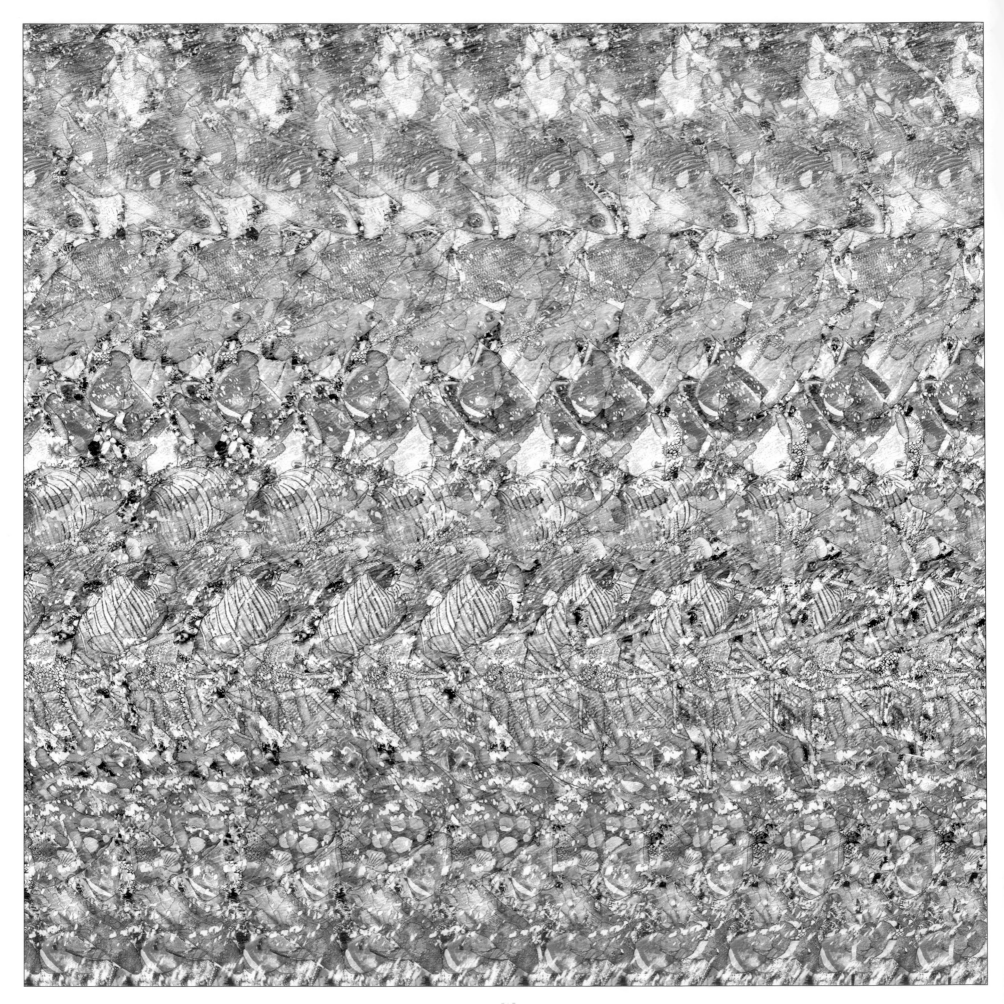

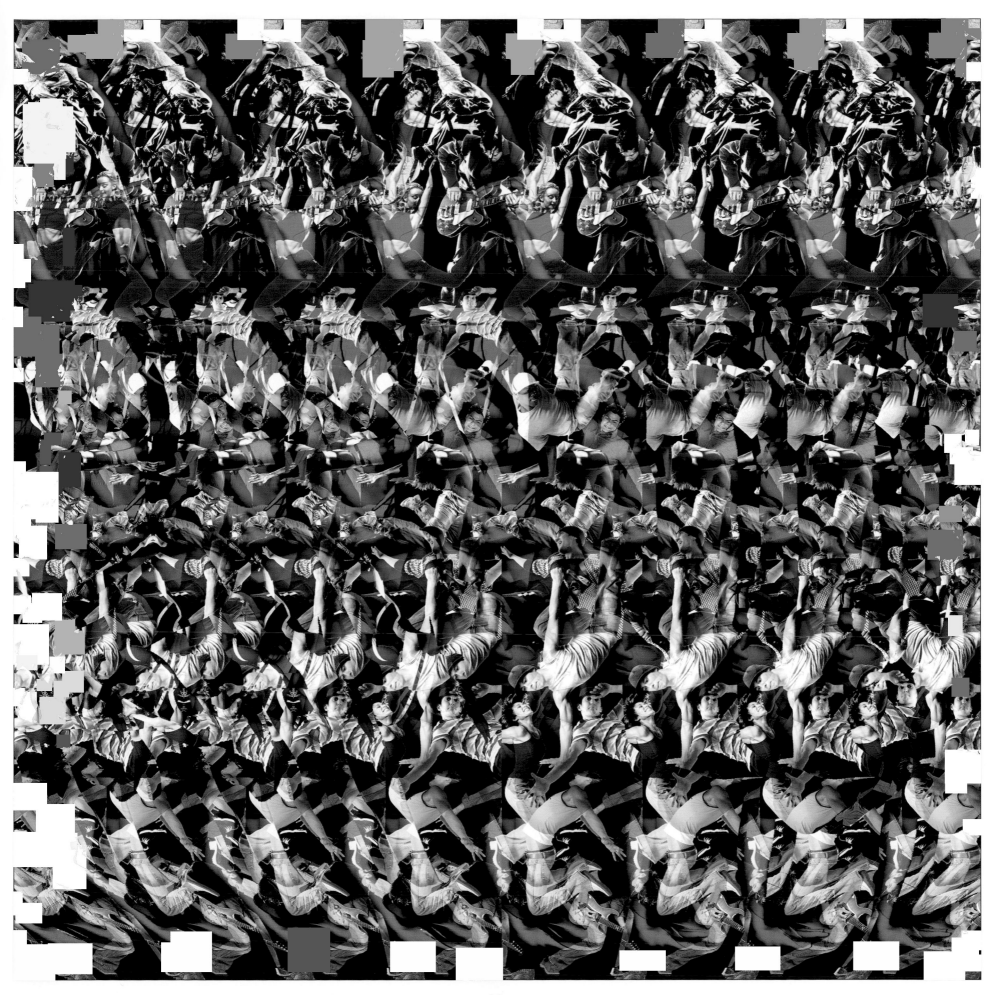

14

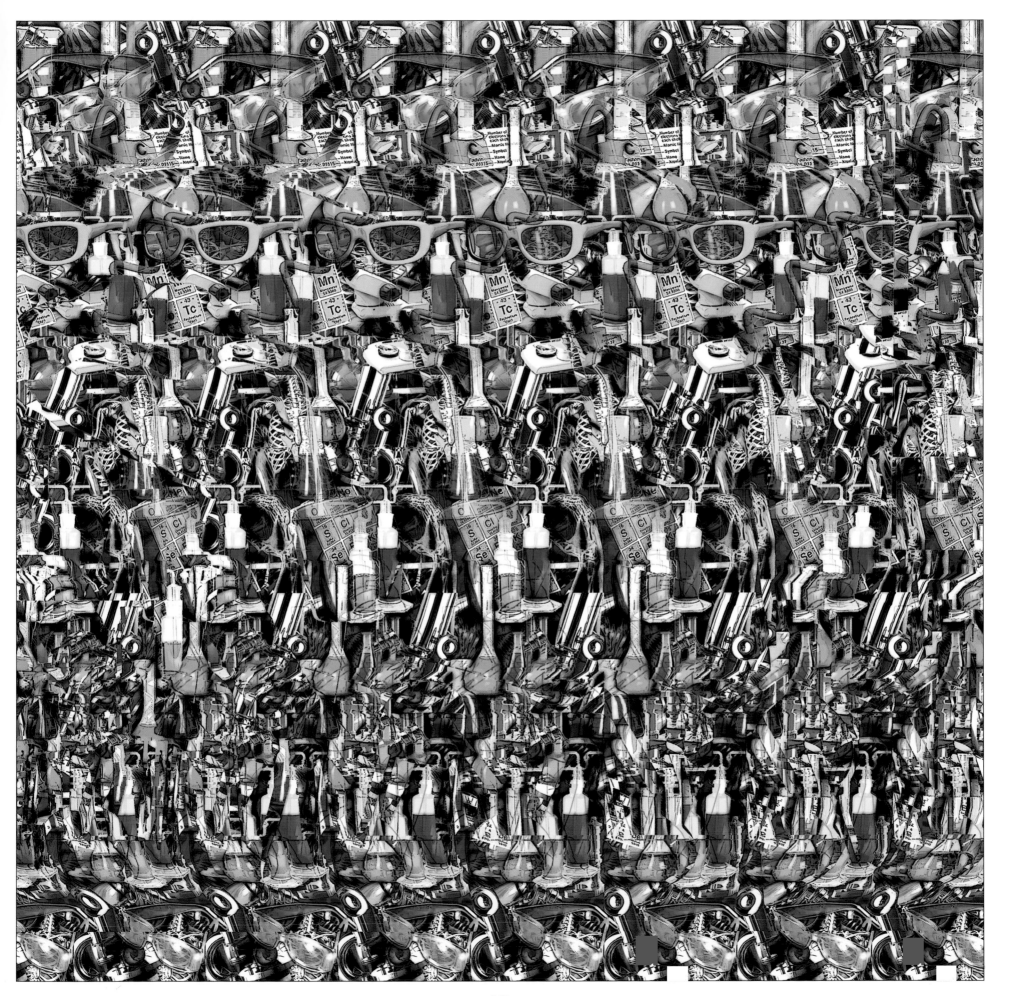

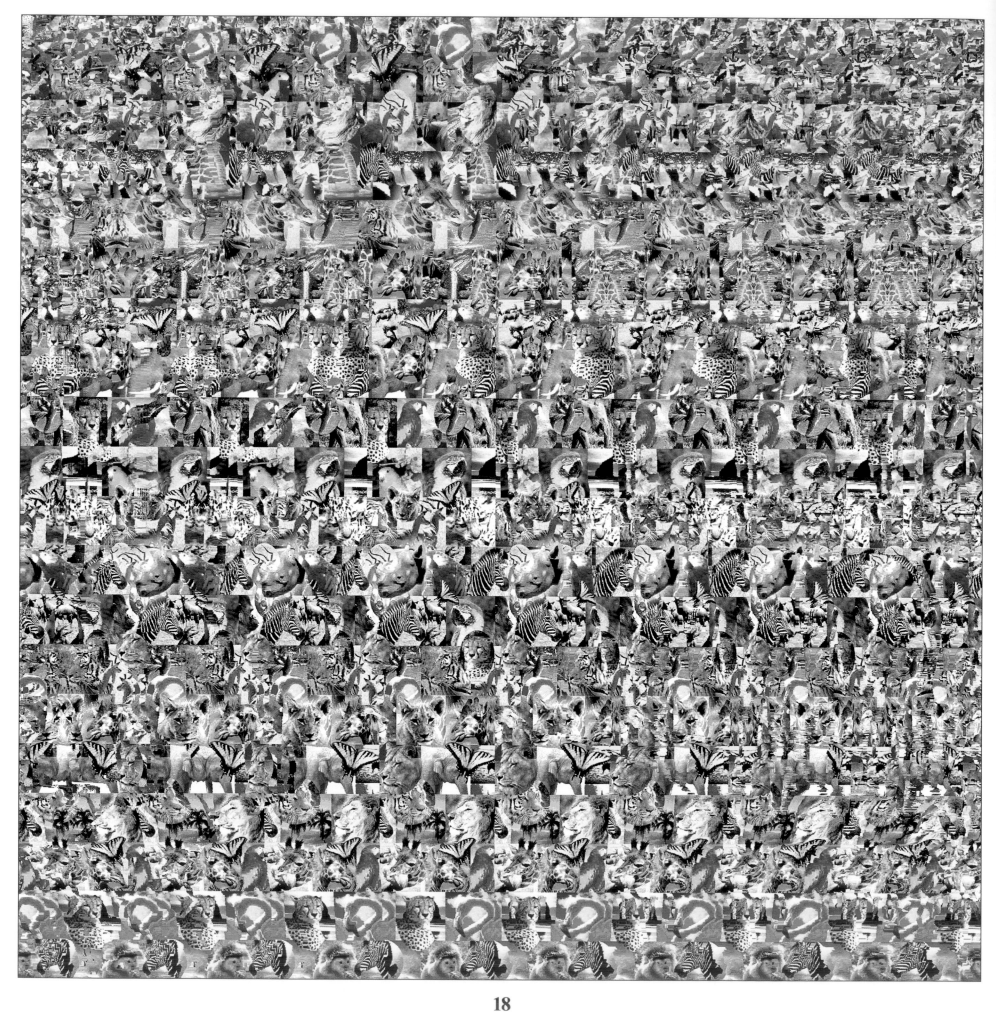

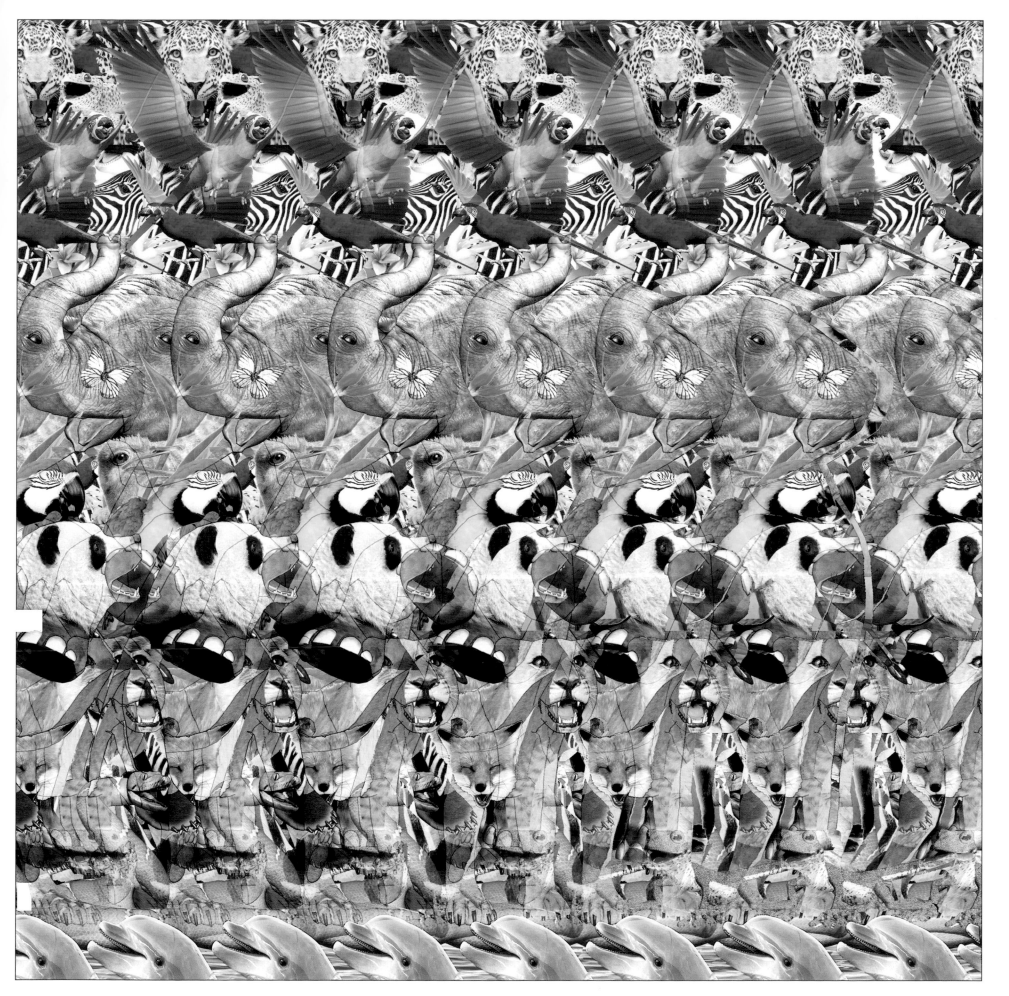

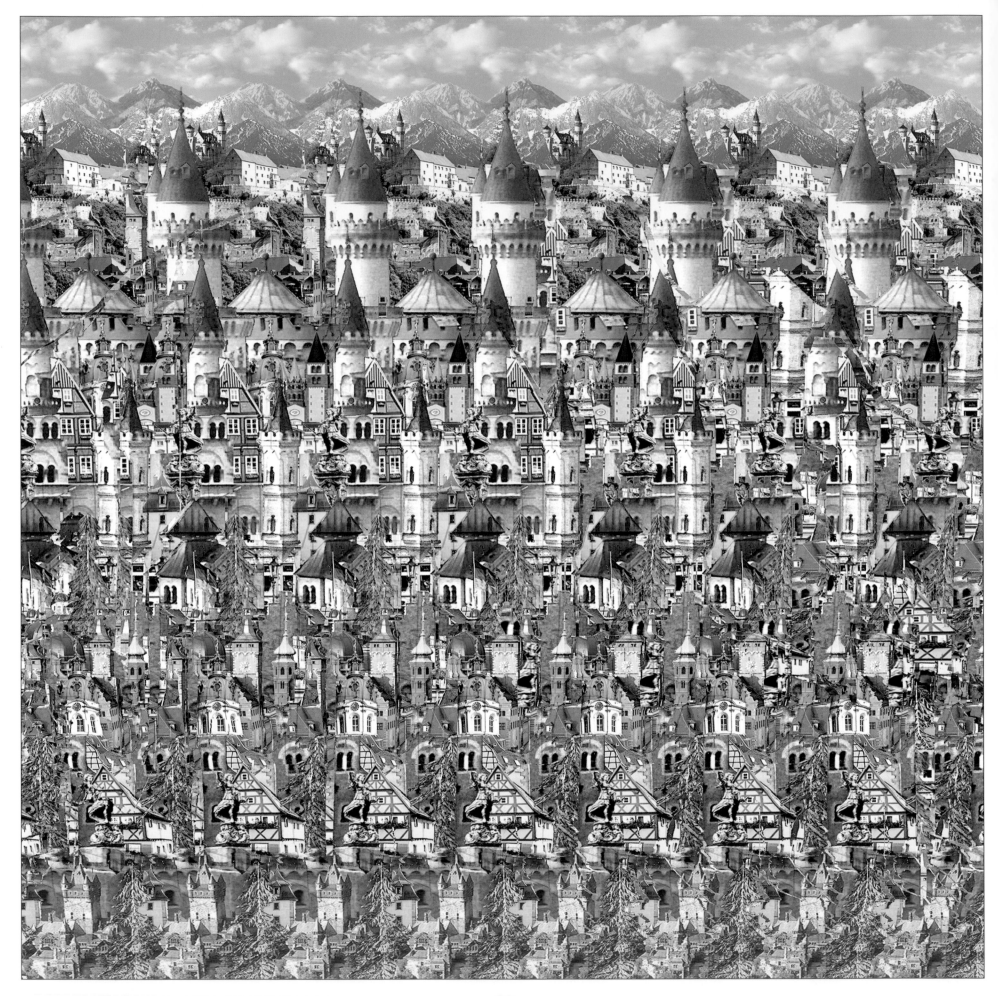

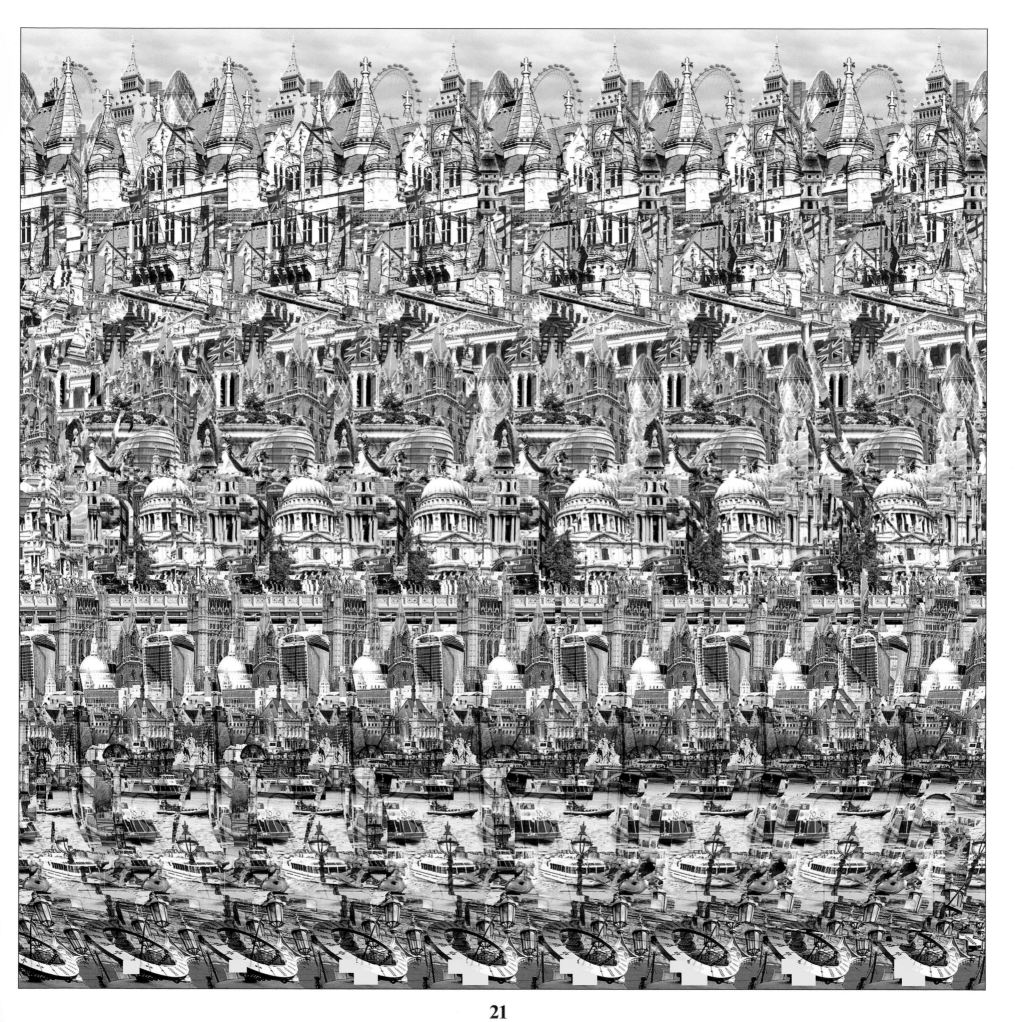

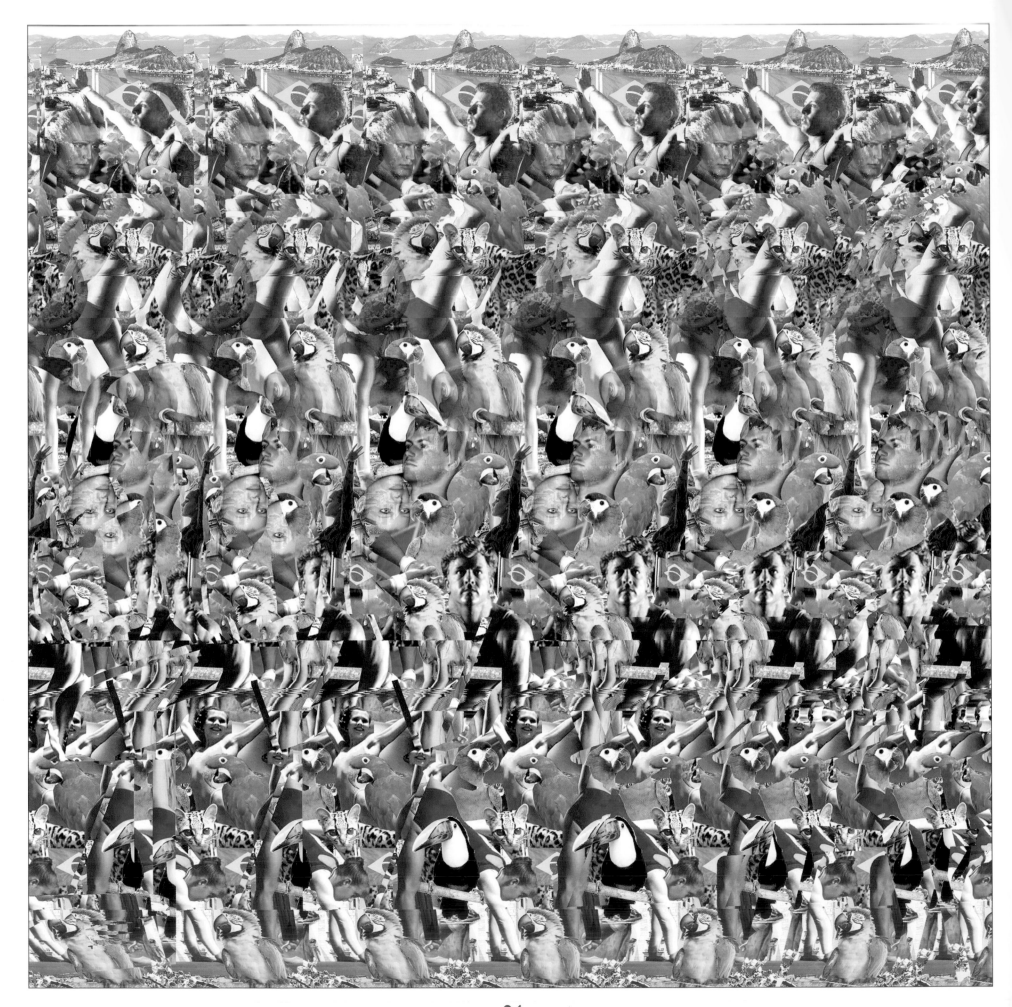

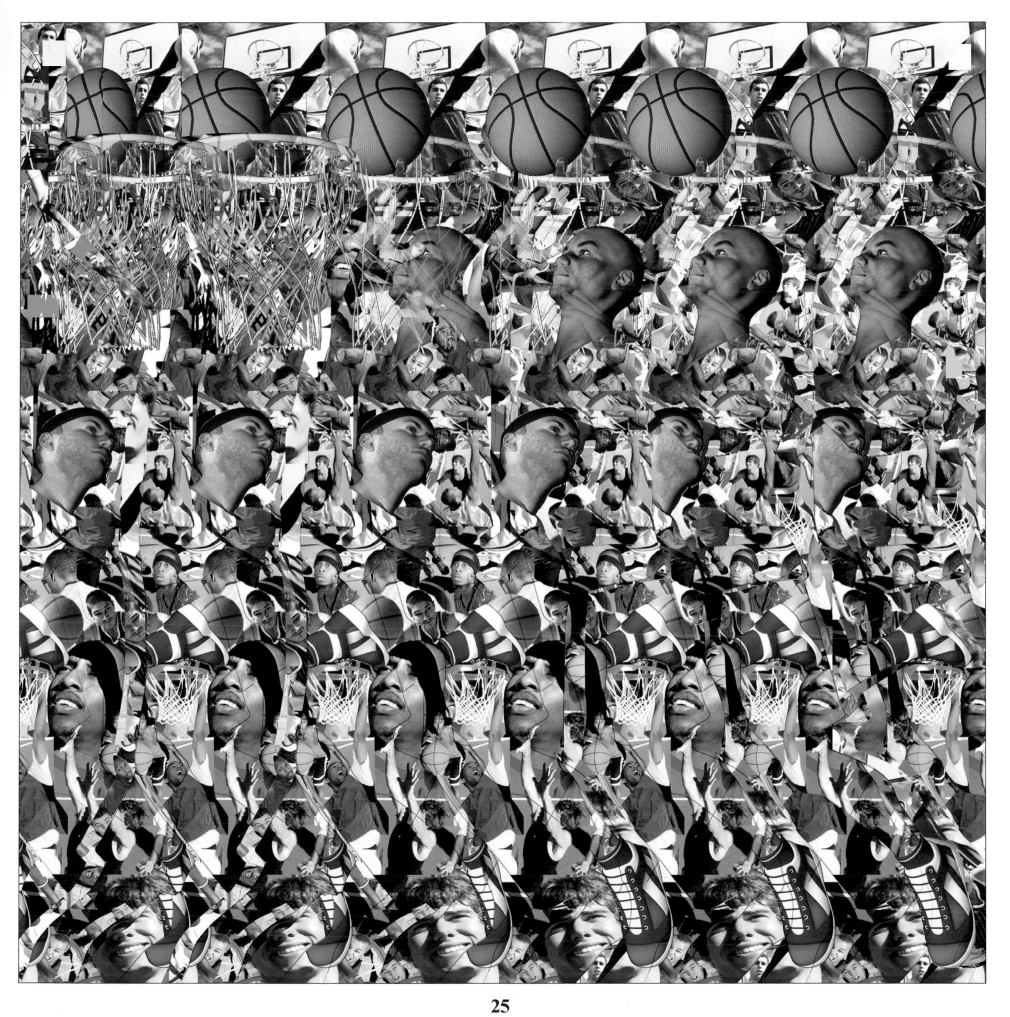

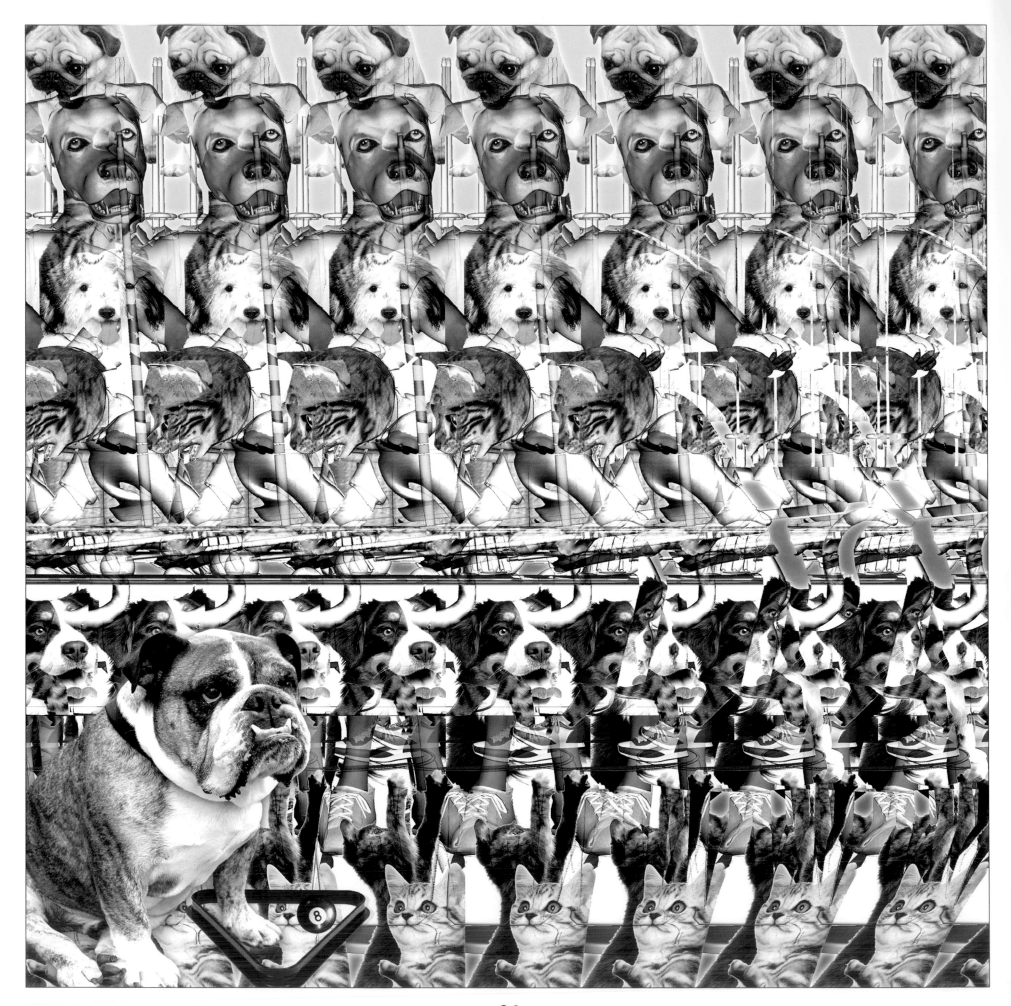

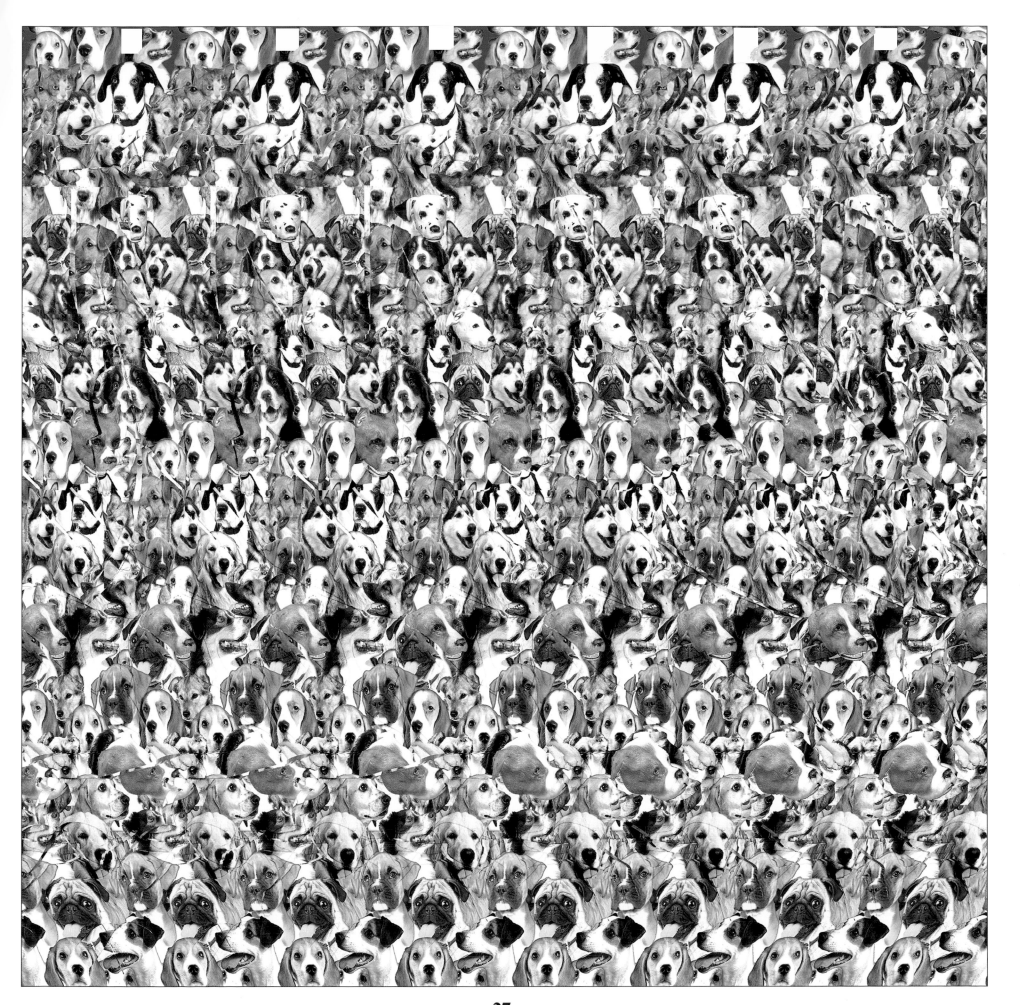

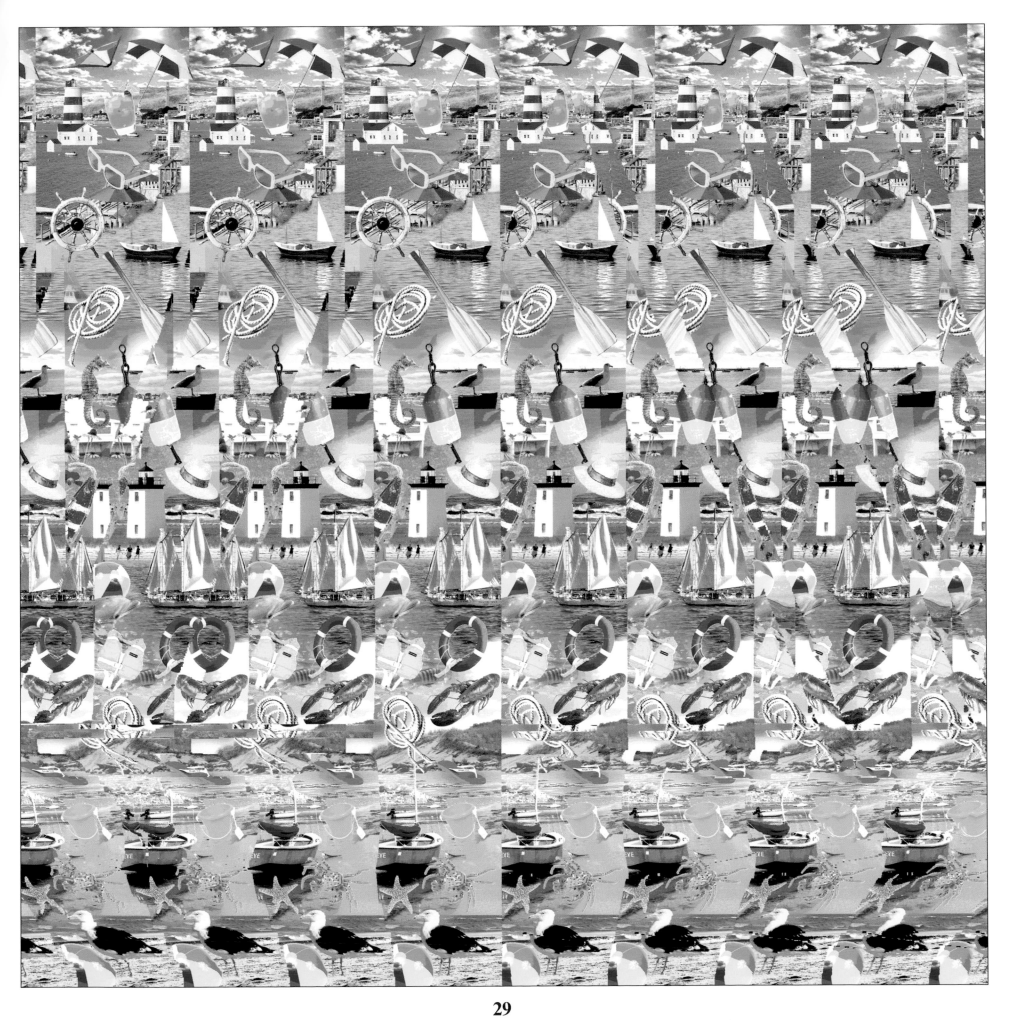

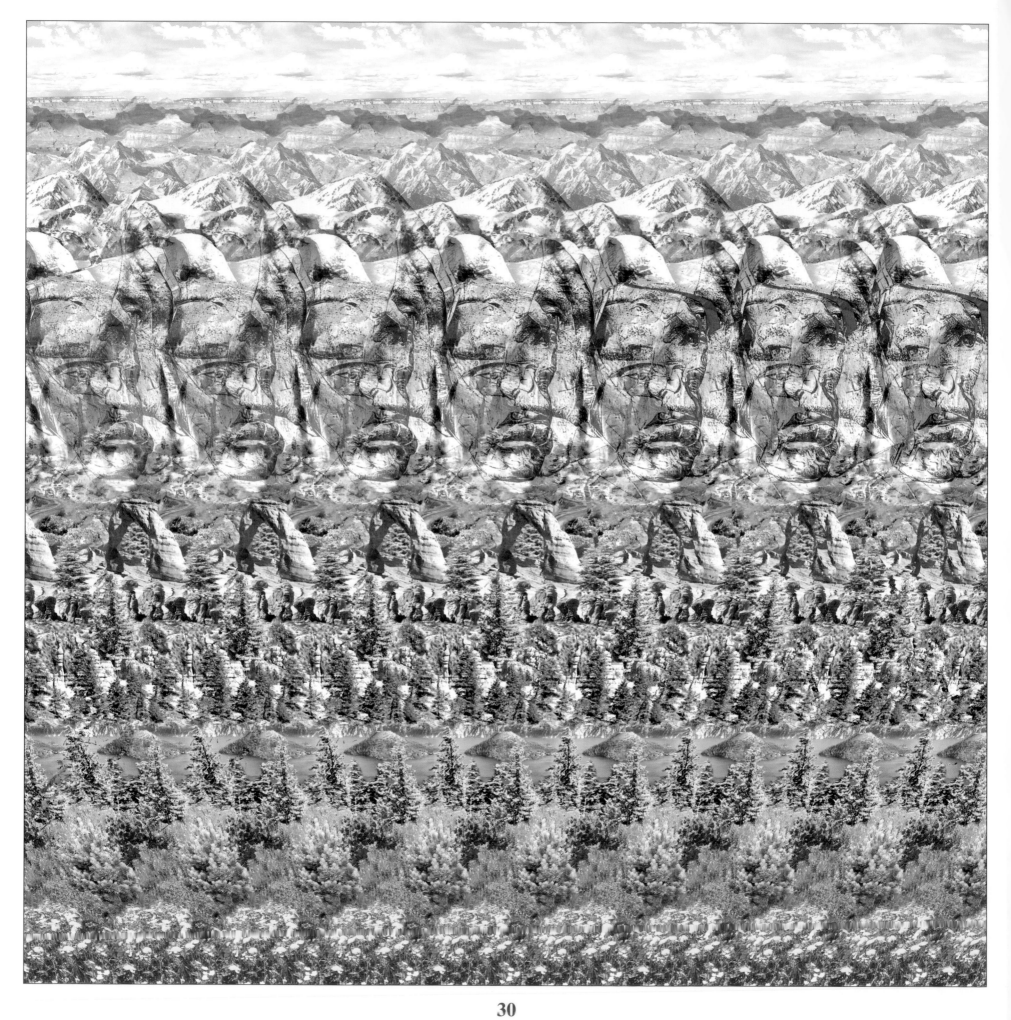

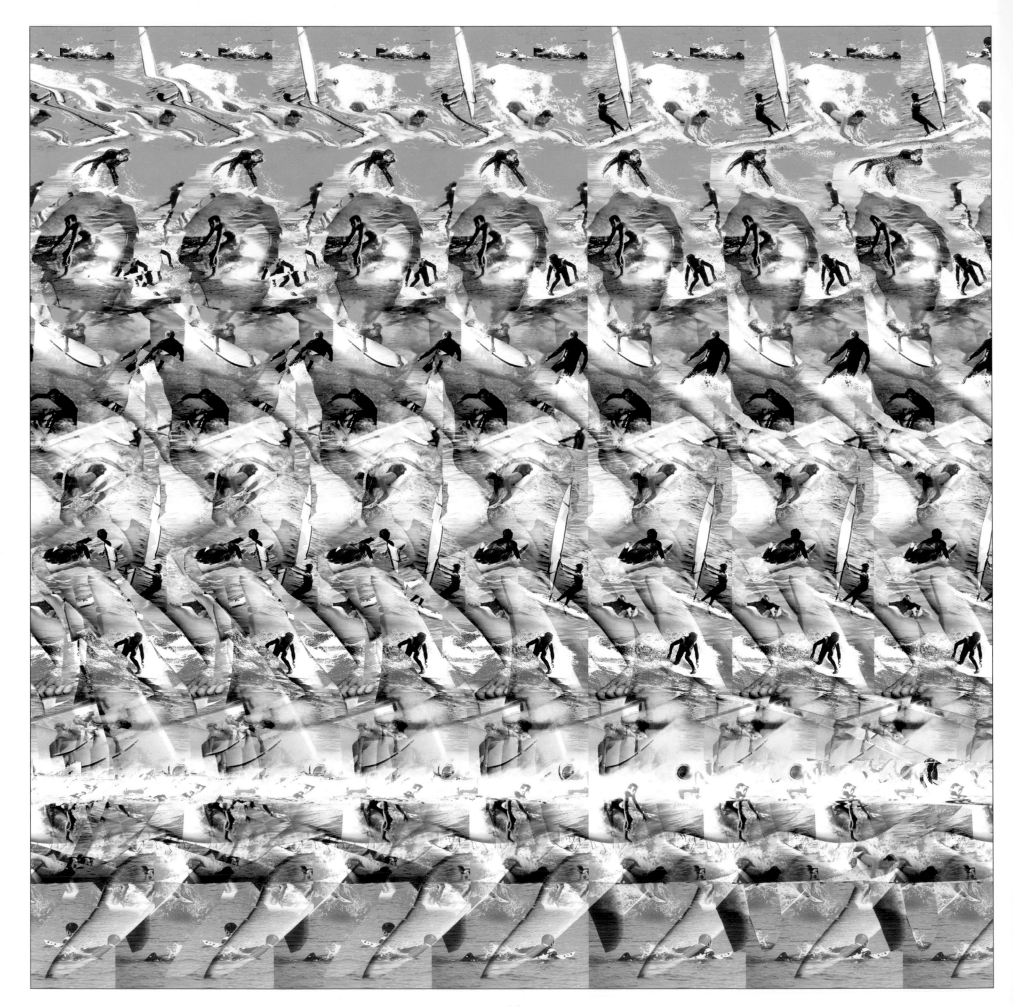

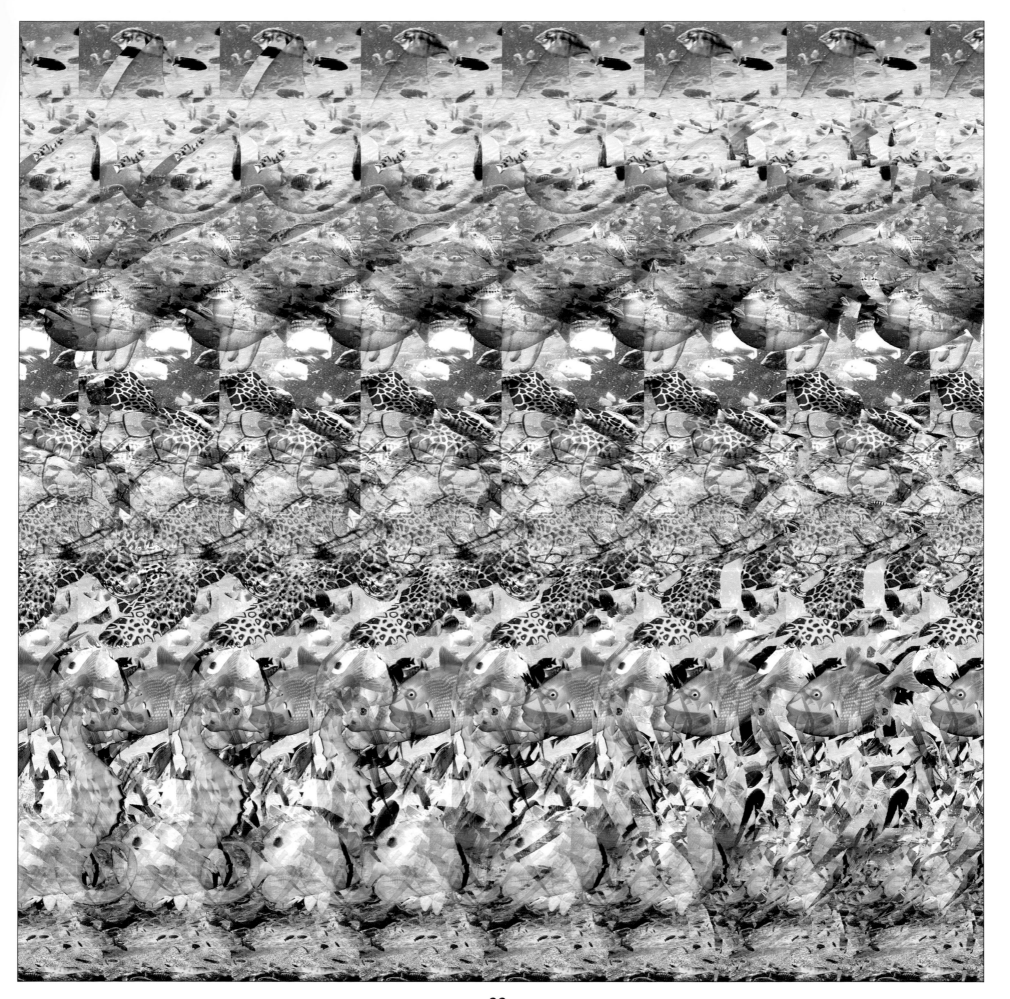

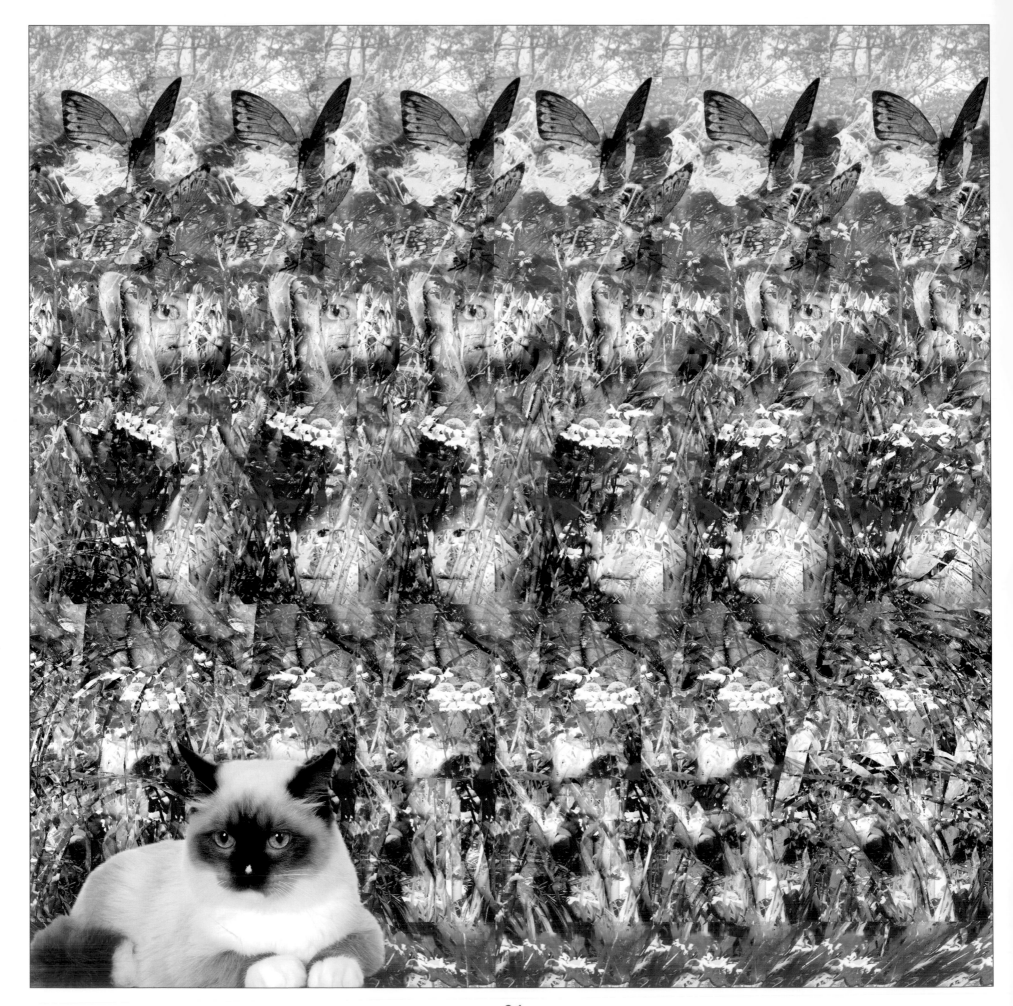

34

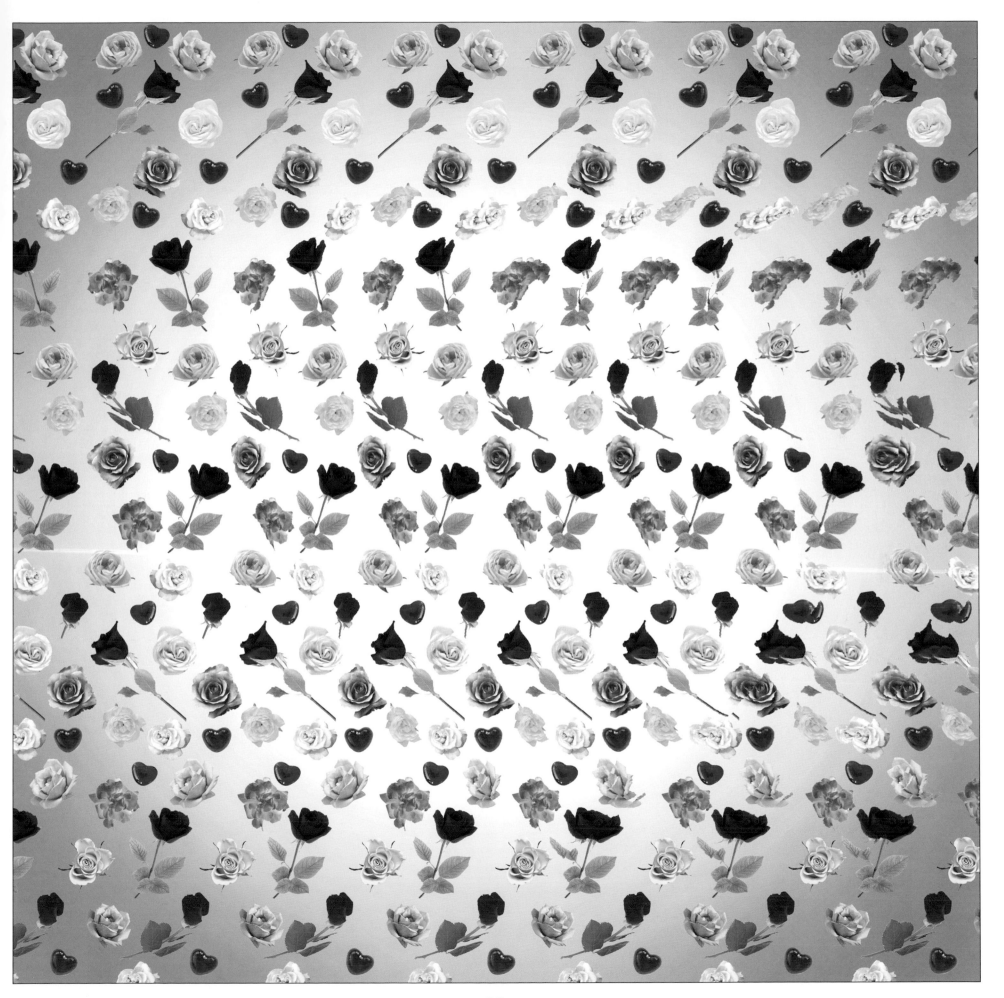

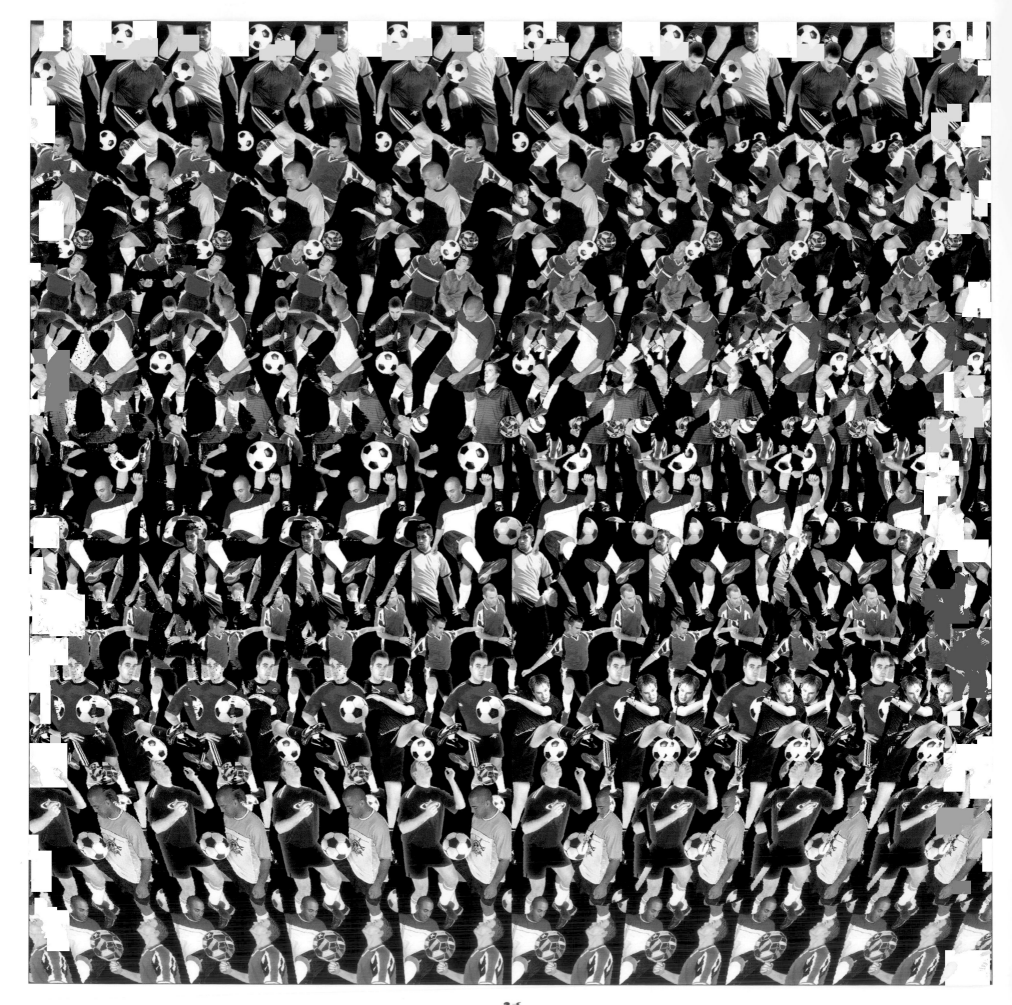

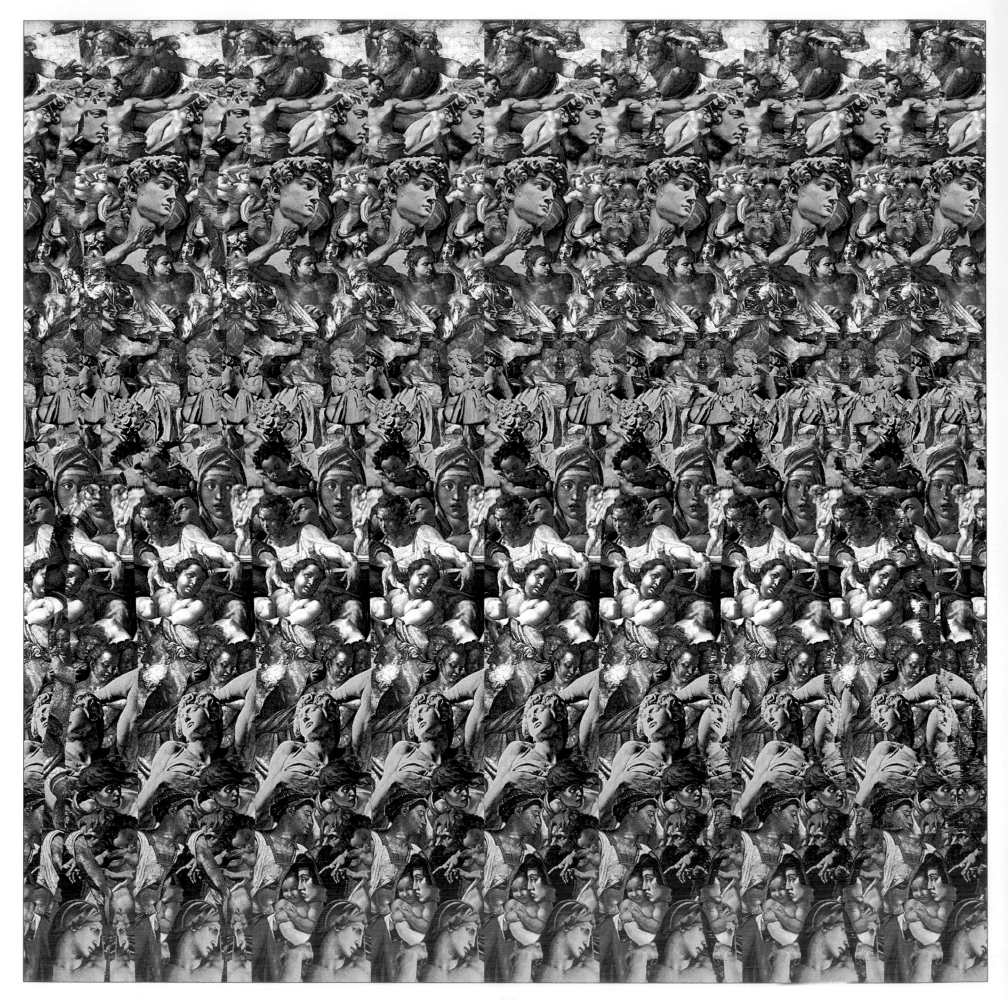

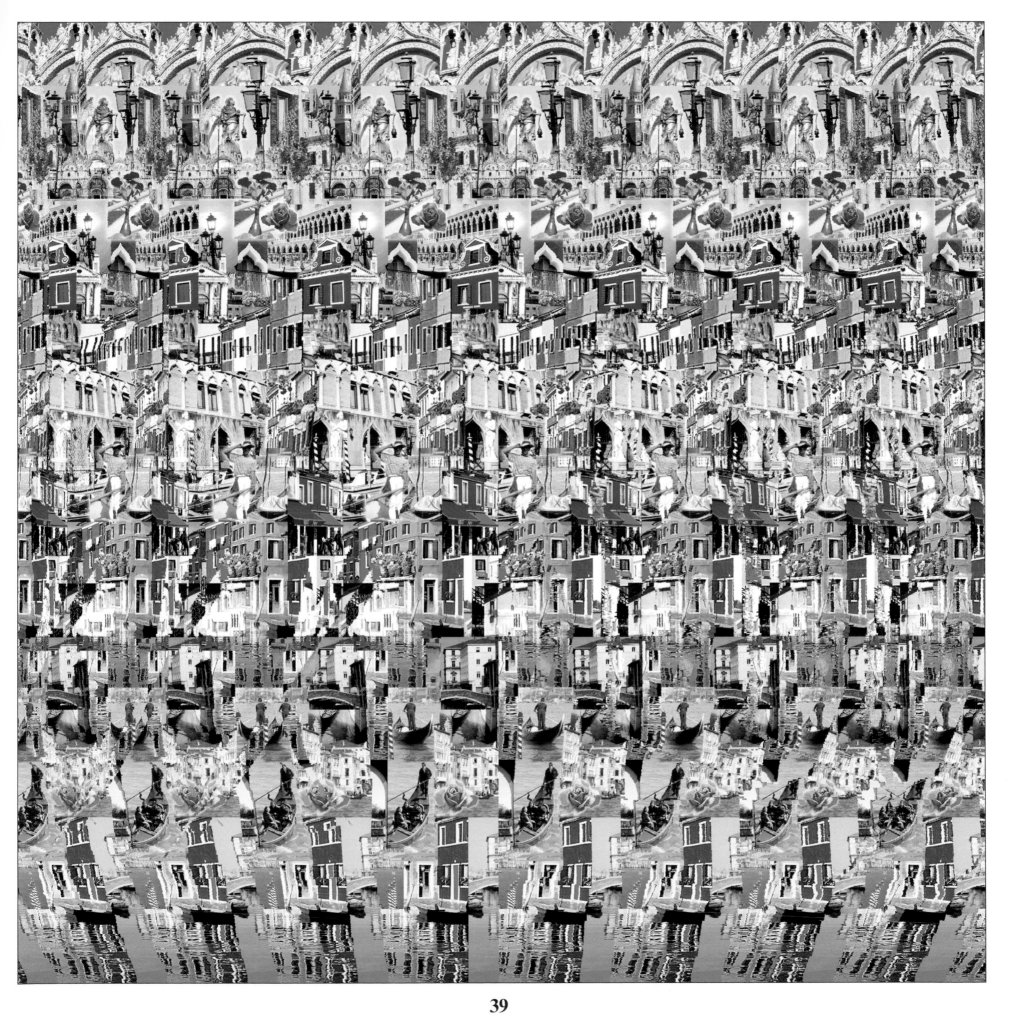

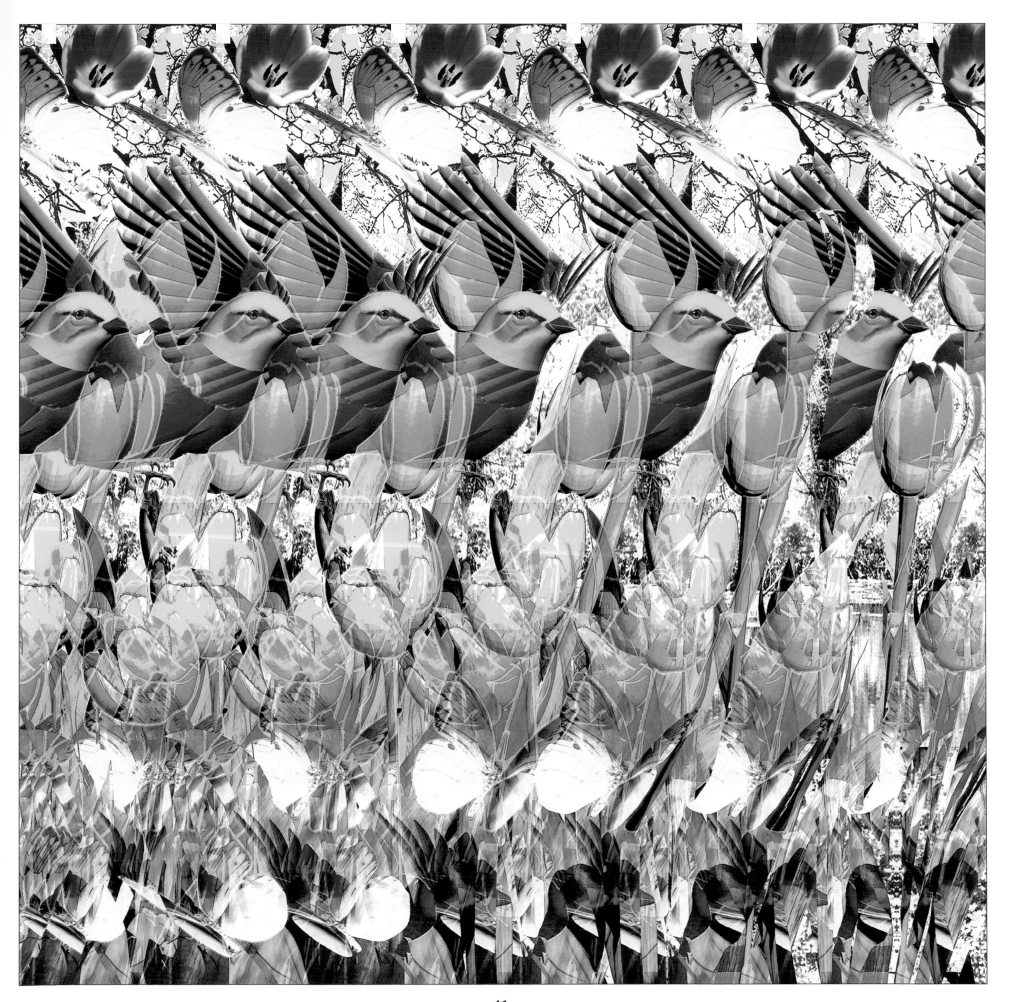

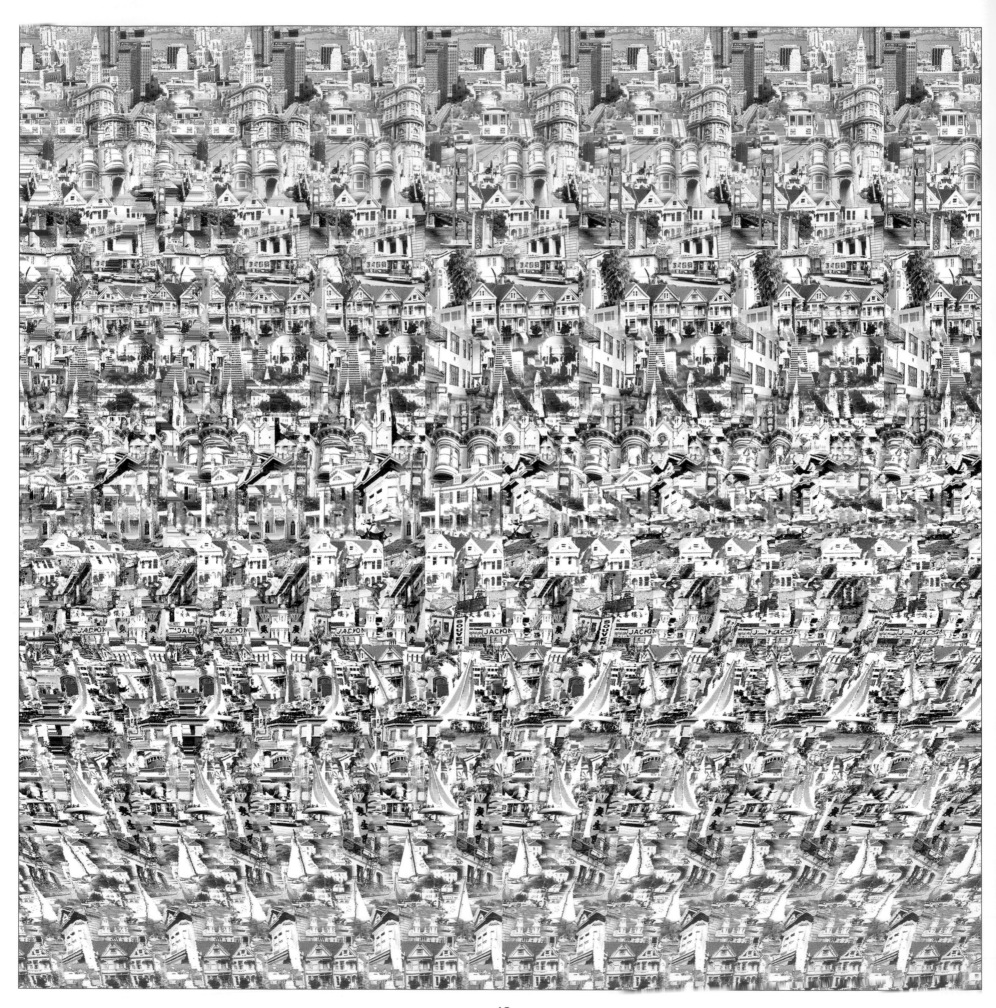

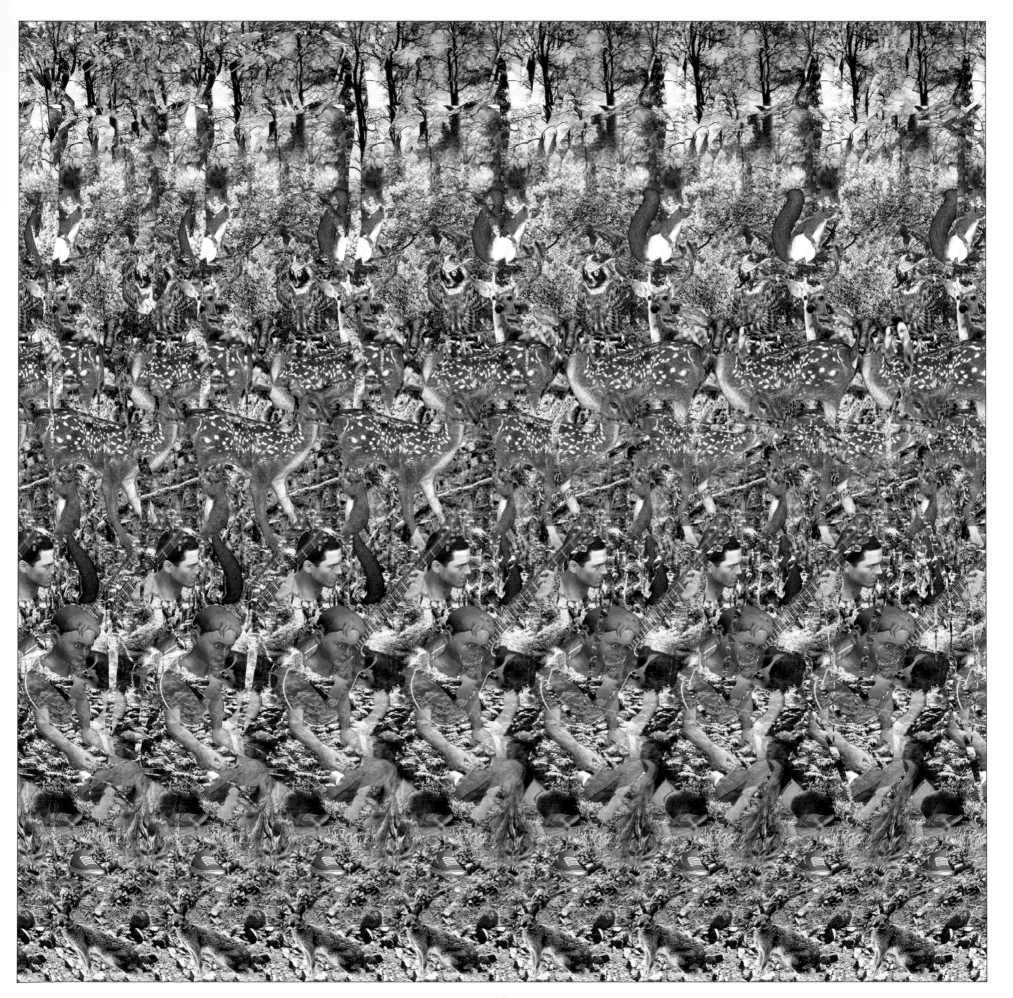

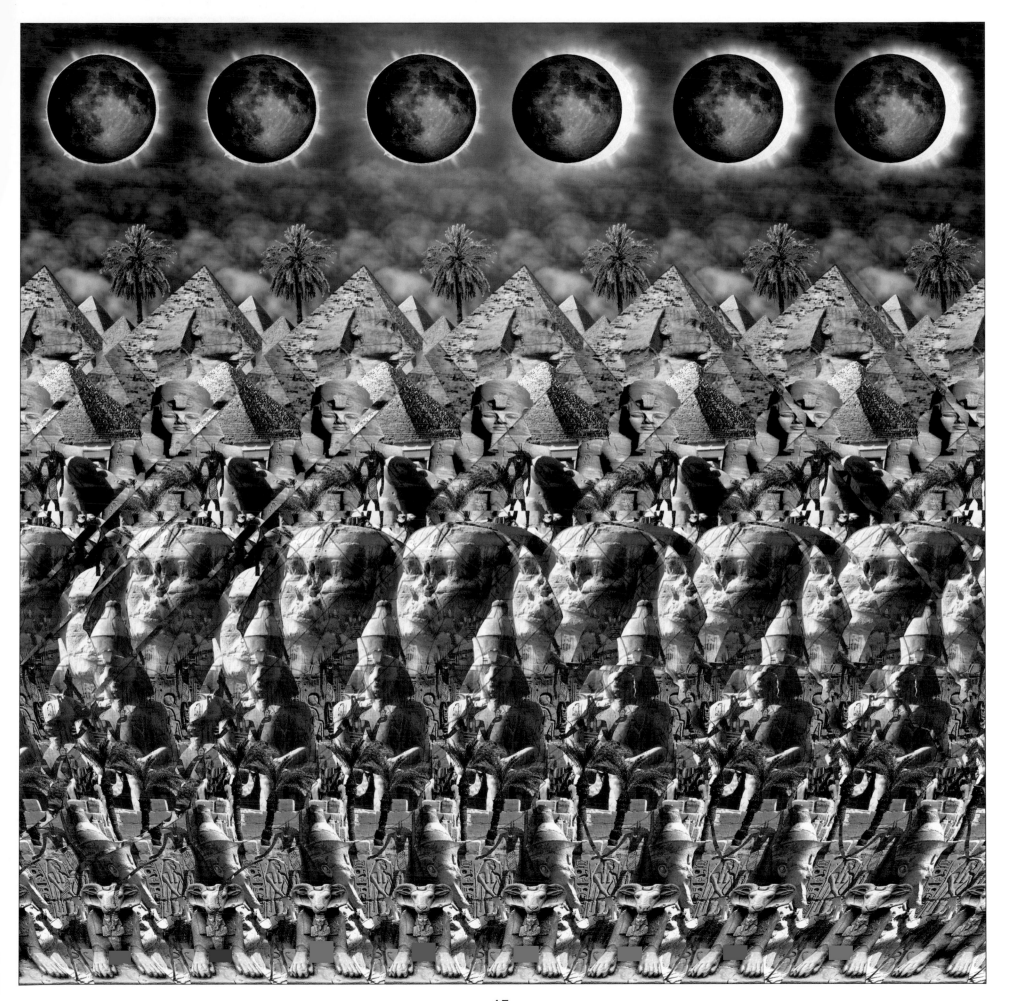

45

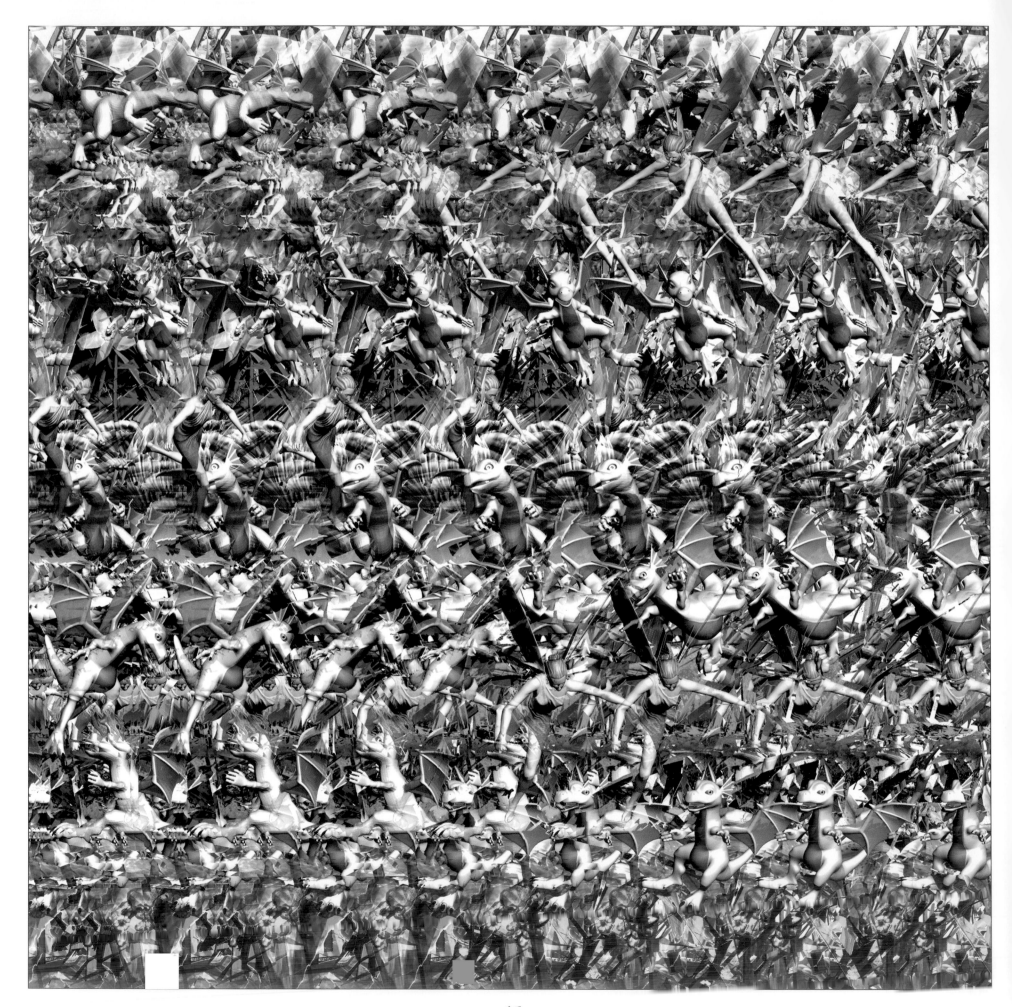

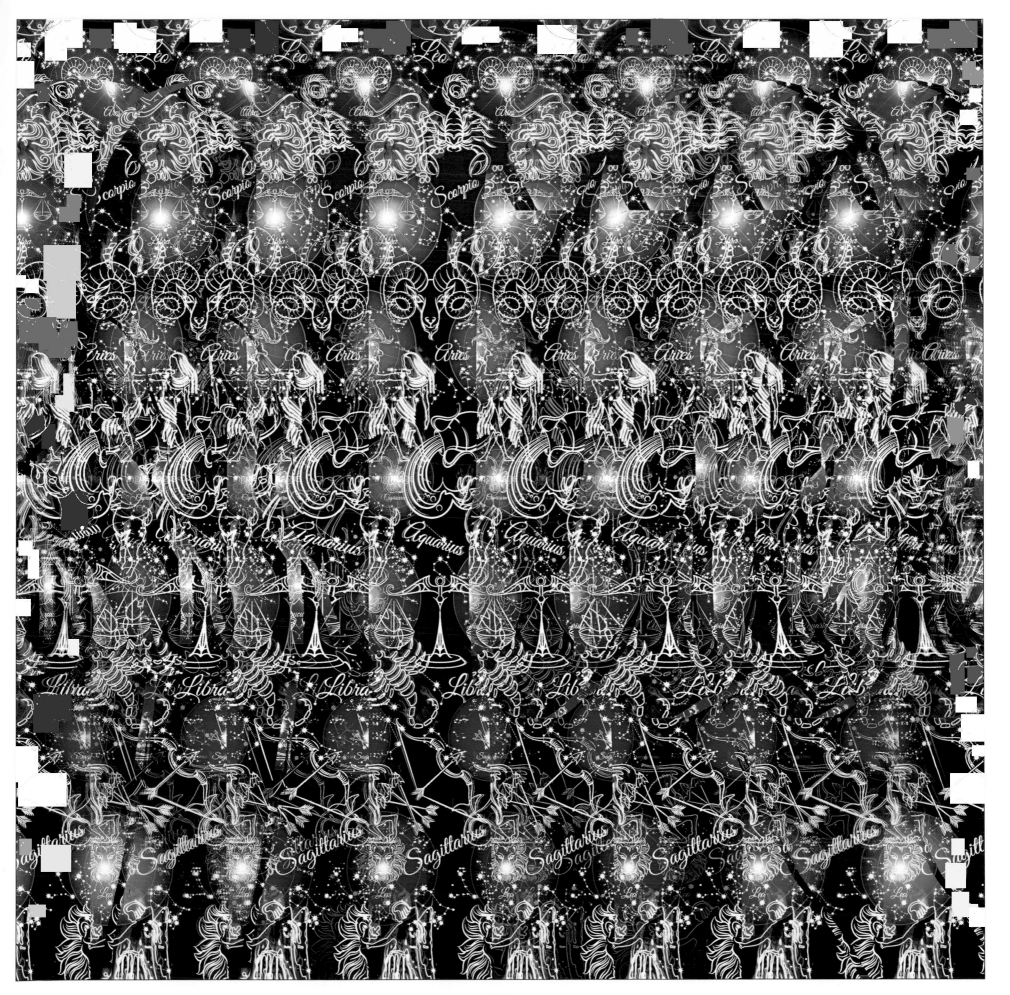

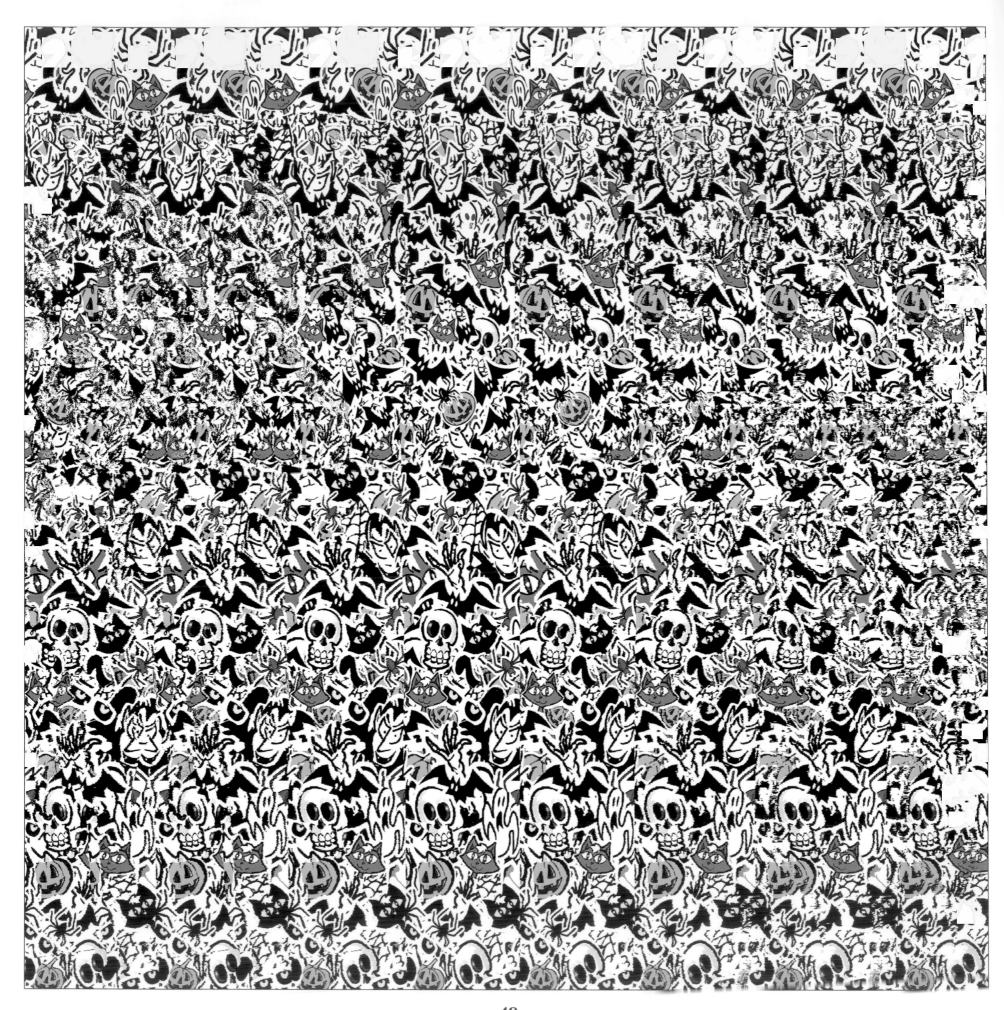

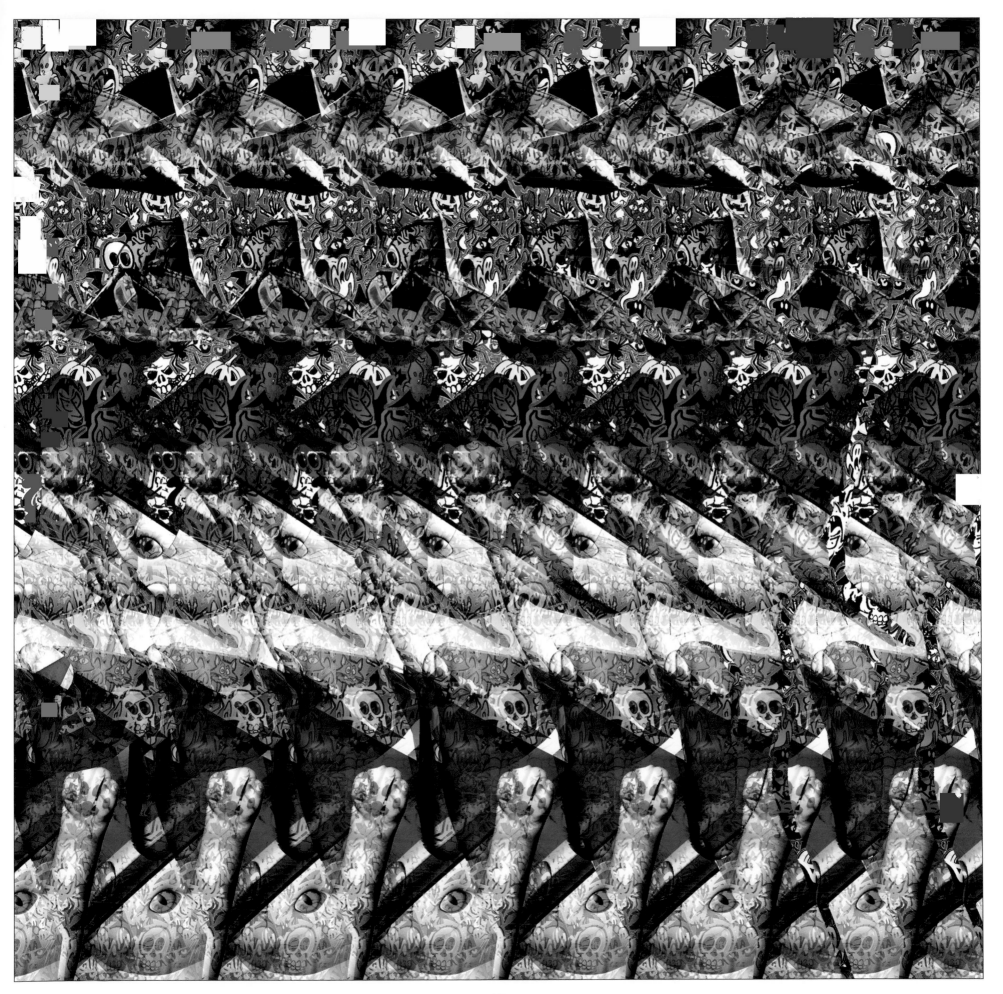

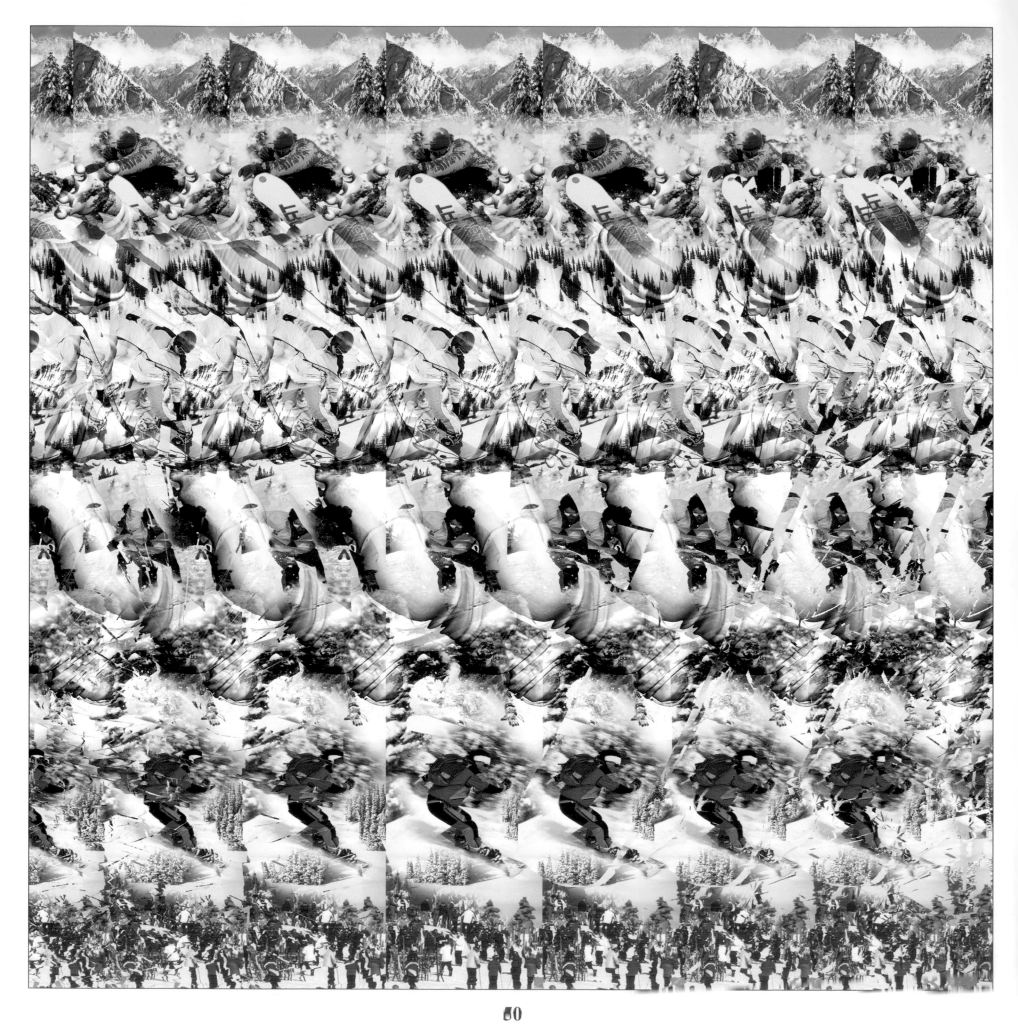

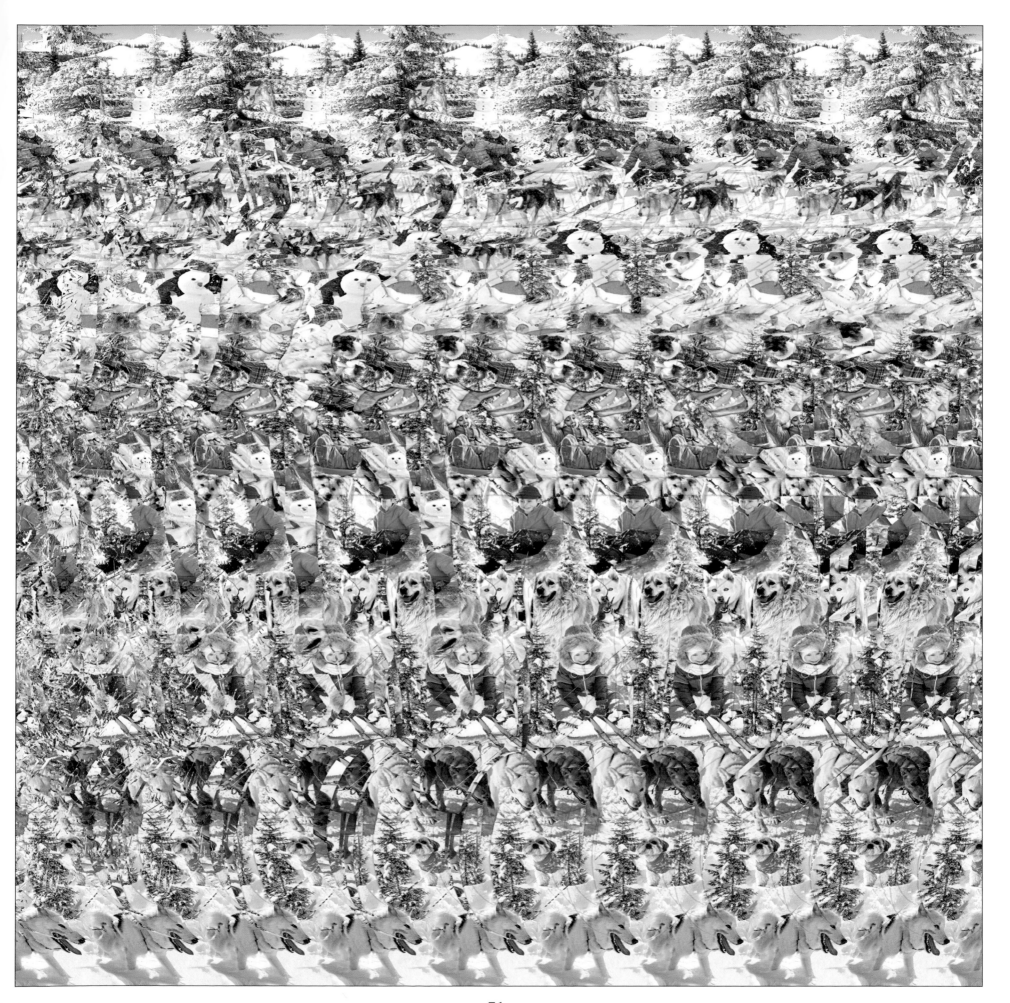

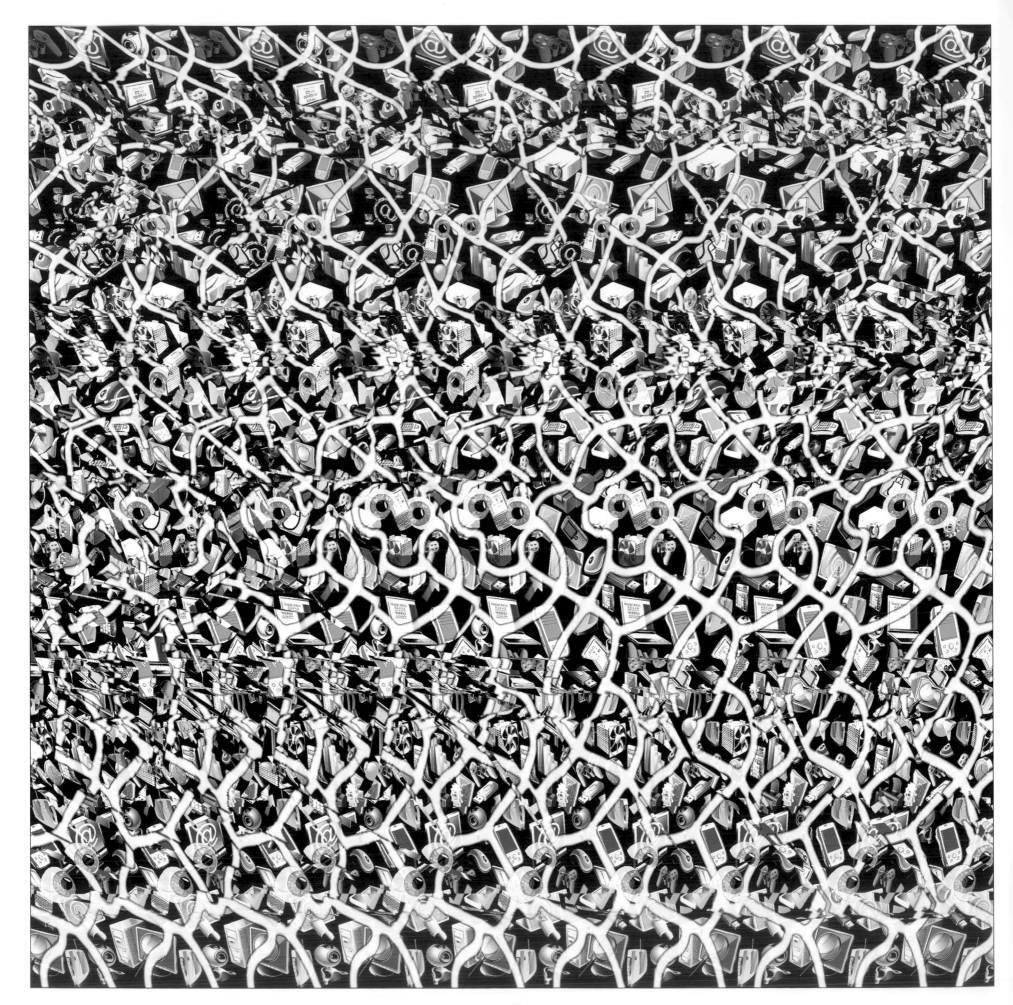

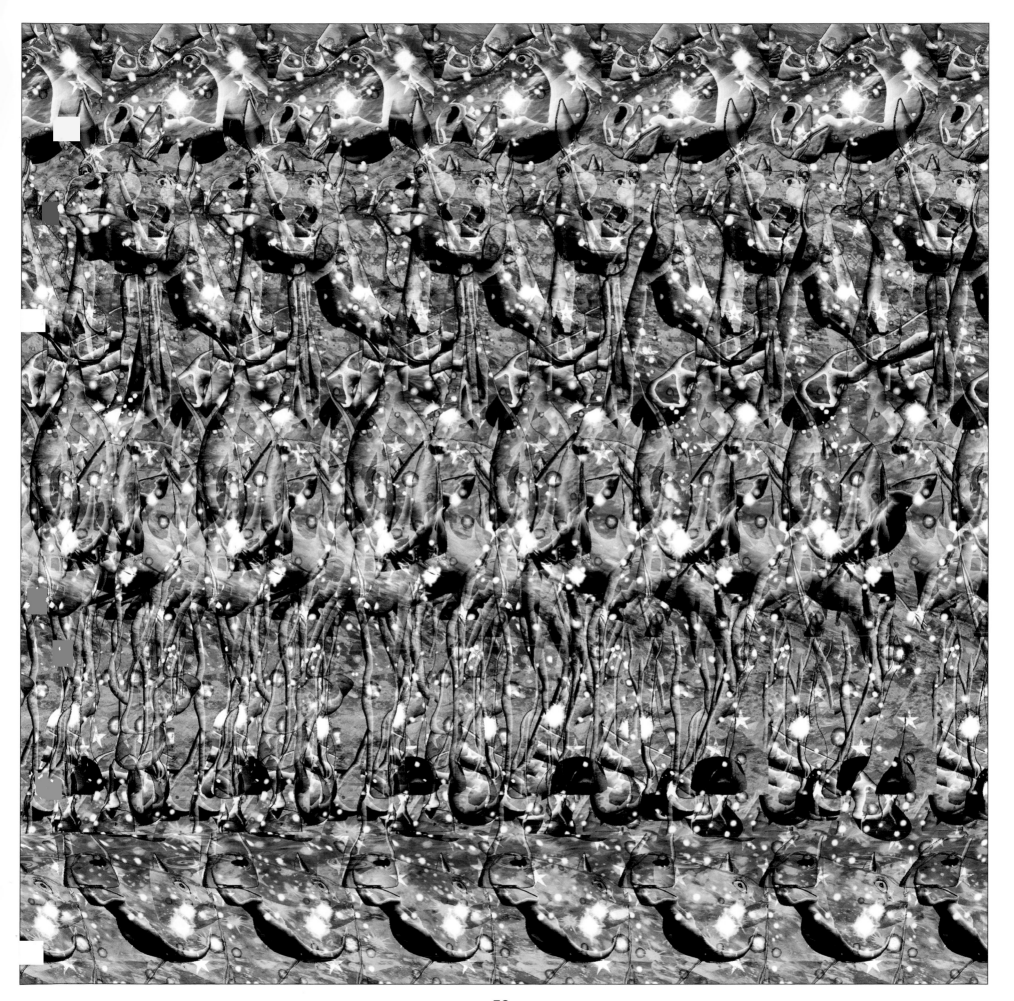

Cover
Manhattan Skyline

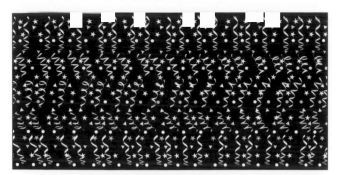

End Pages
Confetti

Page 4
Viewing Techniques

Page 5
Fetch

Page 6
Party Animals

Page 7
Ocean View

Page 8
Rock Star

Page 9
Touchdown Pass

Page 10
Poker Face

Page 11
Yosemite
National Park

Page 12
Sunlit Reef

Page 13
Just Dance

Page 14
Hollywood

Page 15
Invisible

Page 16
Boston Public
Garden

Page 17
The Mulberry Tree

Page 18
Animal Kingdom

Page 19
LOL

Page 20
Neuschwanstein Castle
(Bavaria, Germany)

Page 21
Tower Bridge
(London, England)

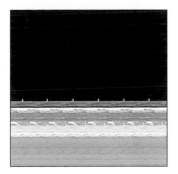

Page 22
Summer Breeze

Page 23
Summer in Paradise

Page 24
Gymnastics

Page 25
Game On

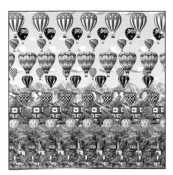

Page 26
NOW You Can
Scratch

Page 27
Who's at the Door?

Page 28
Sandbars & Sunsets

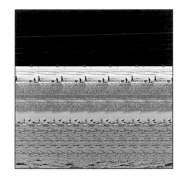

Page 29
Cape Cod

Page 30
Mount Rushmore

Page 31
Up, Up & Away

Page 32
Great Surfing

Page 33
Tag, You're It

Page 34
Jumping into Spring

Page 35
Love Is in the Air

Page 36
Soccer Star

Page 37
Just for Kicks

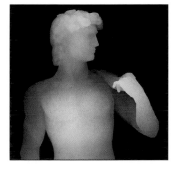

Page 38
Michelangelo's *David*

Page 39
Venice (Italy)

Page 40
Tropical Retreat

Page 41
Flying into Spring

Page 42
Golden Gate Bridge

Page 43
Happy Camper

Page 44
Brandenburg Gate
(Berlin, Germany)

Page 45
Solar Eclipse

Page 46
Dragonflies

Page 47
Aries the Ram
(Zodiac Sign)

Page 48
Mummy

Page 49
Cat & Bats

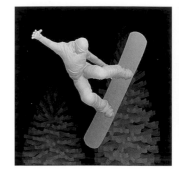

Page 50
Hotshot

Page 51
Dog Sledding

Page 52
Surfing the Web

Page 53
Nightmare